T. Alfred Stowell

The Church Catechism

With Explanations, Notes, and Proofs from Scripture

T. Alfred Stowell

The Church Catechism
With Explanations, Notes, and Proofs from Scripture

ISBN/EAN: 9783743686717

Printed in Europe, USA, Canada, Australia, Japan

Cover: Foto ©Lupo / pixelio.de

More available books at **www.hansebooks.com**

THE CHURCH CATECHISM

WITH

EXPLANATIONS, NOTES, AND PROOFS
FROM SCRIPTURE

For the Use of Teachers and Students

BY

T. ALFRED STOWELL, M.A.

QUEEN'S COLLEGE, OXFORD; RECTOR OF CHORLEY; HON. CANON OF MANCHESTER
CATHEDRAL; AND RURAL DEAN OF LEYLAND

London
JAMES NISBET & CO.
21 BERNERS STREET
1894

PREFACE.

THE special feature which characterises this little book is the frequent use of comparisons with, and illustrations drawn from, the Baptismal Offices, the Articles of Religion, and Dean Nowell's Catechisms.* The references to the Bible have been very carefully selected, and are in many cases to be regarded not merely as proofs, but also as forming part of the explanation designed to be given.

---

* Nowell's Catechism was unanimously approved and allowed by the Lower House of Convocation in 1562 ("a tribute of respect which confers on it a species of semi-authority"—Bishop Short); and the intention appears to have been entertained to give it and Jewell's "Apology" an authority similar to that of the XXXIX. Articles, by uniting them in one book, which should be set forth as containing the true doctrine of the Church of England. This intention was not carried out; but the Synod of 1603 has given to both Catechisms all the authority with which that body could invest them, for there is no doubt that they are referred to in the 79th Canon, which directs that "all schoolmasters shall teach in English or Latin, as the children are able to hear, the Larger or Shorter Catechism, heretofore by public authority set forth."

To show the importance and authority of Nowell's Catechisms, it may be sufficient to quote the memoir (p. vii.) in the Parker Society's reprint: "We may judge of the high estimation in which these works were held, when we learn from the various 'Injunctions,' &c., put forth at that time by public authorities, that no Catechisms were allowed to be used by clergymen and schoolmasters, except one or other of Nowell's" (Cardwell's "Synodalia," i. 128; Grindal's "Remains," pp. 142, 152).

It has been shown by various writers that the second part of the Catechism relating to the Sacraments was not composed by Dean Overall, but merely edited by him from Nowell's, which had been approved by the Convocations of 1562, 1571, and 1603. Its immediate source was Nowell's "Shorter Catechism," which is distinct from the "Larger" and

Inasmuch as the purpose of the Church Catechism is to give instruction preparatory to Confirmation, and therefore to participation in the Lord's Supper, the writer has thought it allowable to treat that Sacrament somewhat fully.

The writer consciously, and doubtless still more unconsciously, owes much to those who have preceded him in the same field. He desires to acknowledge his special obligation to Dean Vaughan and the late Archdeacon Norris.

He cannot refrain from availing himself of this opportunity of expressing his own great and ever-increasing value of the admirable summary of Christian doctrine and duty furnished in the Church Catechism as a manual for the instruction of the young; and he hopes that this humble attempt to illustrate and explain it may be found useful to this end.

Abbreviations used:—P.B., Book of Common Prayer. P.B.V., Prayer-Book Version. R.V., Revised Version of 1881. Bapt. Ser., Baptismal Service. Art., Article of Religion. Nowell's Cat., Nowell's Catechism.

---

the "Middle" Catechisms, which are better known; the former having been published by the Parker Society in 1853, and the latter by the Prayer-Book and Homily Society in 1851.

Copies of this "Shorter Catechism" are extremely rare. It was reprinted in Dublin by M'Gee in 1878, but is now out of print, the writer having secured the last copy.

See Preface to Jacobson's edition of Nowell's "Larger Catechism," in Latin. Oxford, 1844.

CONTENTS.

	PAGE
PREFACE	v

INTRODUCTION :—

The Design of the Catechism	1
History of the Catechism	2
Plan of the Catechism	2

PART I.

THE CHRISTIAN COVENANT	4
1. Christian Privileges	5
2. Christian Duties	9

PART II.

THE CHRISTIAN'S RULE OF FAITH—THE CREED	19
Summary of its Teaching	32

PART III.

THE CHRISTIAN'S RULE OF LIFE	38
The Ten Commandments	40
Duty towards God	40
Duty towards my Neighbour	48

PART IV.

THE CHRISTIAN'S RESOURCE—PRAYER	57
The Lord's Prayer	59

PART V.

THE SACRAMENTS	67
The Sacrament of Baptism	72
The Sacrament of the Lord's Supper	79

QUESTIONS 92

THE CHURCH CATECHISM.

INTRODUCTION.

A CATECHISM is a course of instruction by means of questions and answers.*

"The Church Catechism" (Ministration of Public Baptism of Infants) is such a course of instruction in the first principles or elementary truths of the Christian religion.† It is especially intended to teach children their *duty* as Christians—that is, to explain the nature of the promises made in their name at their baptism. It is therefore described in the title prefixed to it as "An Instruction to be learned of every person before he be brought to be confirmed by the Bishop."

In "The Ministration of Public Baptism of Infants," the godparents are thus exhorted : "Ye must remember that it is your parts and duties to see that this infant be taught, so soon as he shall be able to learn, what a solemn vow, promise, and profession he hath here made by you ;" and "*that he may know these things the better* . . . chiefly ye shall provide that he may learn the Creed, the Lord's Prayer, and the Ten Commandments in the vulgar tongue (the English language), and all other things which a Christian ought to know and believe to his soul's health;" and again, "Ye are to take care that this child be brought to the Bishop to be confirmed of him so soon as he can say the Creed, the Lord's Prayer, and the Ten Commandments in the vulgar tongue, *and be further instructed in the Church Catechism set forth* (appointed and published) *for that purpose.*"

In the Preface to "The Order of Confirmation" it is declared, "To the

---

* The name comes from the Greek word which is translated in St. Luke i. 4, "instructed" (also in Acts xviii. 25). It literally means to "sound down," or "in one's ears"—to teach by word of mouth.

† In Canon 60 it is called "The Catechism of the Christian Religion."

A

end that Confirmation may be ministered to the more edifying of such as shall receive it, the Church hath thought good to order that none hereafter shall be confirmed but such as can say the Creed, the Lord's Prayer, and the Ten Commandments, *and can also answer to such other questions as in the Short Catechism are contained;* to the end that children being now come to the years of discretion, and *having learned what their godfathers and godmothers promised for them in Baptism*, they may themselves, with their own mouth and consent, openly before the Church, ratify and confirm the same," &c.

In Canon 61 it is "ordered that none shall be presented for Confirmation but such as can *render an account of their faith*, according to the Catechism." *

The duty of parents and masters to see that their children learn, and are instructed in, this Catechism, and of the parochial clergy to instruct and examine the children of the parish in the same, is set forth in the Rubrics at the end of the Catechism.†

History.—The first Prayer-Book of Edward VI. (A.D. 1549) contained the Catechism as far as the explanation of the Lord's Prayer, with only a few verbal alterations from its present form. Until 1661 this was placed in the Order of Confirmation ("wherein is contained a Catechism for children"). The explanation of the Sacraments was added in the reign of James I. after the Hampton Court Conference in 1604, and was probably taken from the "Little Catechism" of Dean Nowell.

The **Plan of the Catechism** is very simple. It takes us back to our Baptism, and unfolds the nature of the Christian Covenant—the Covenant between God and man in Christ—into which we were then admitted. First, it declares its privileges—the promises made by God in Christ in the Gospel, and "visibly signed and sealed" to us in that Sacrament "wherein I was made a member of Christ, the child of God, and an inheritor of the kingdom of heaven." Secondly, it declares its duties—the promises which we then made by our sureties, repentance or renunciation, faith, and obedience, and our obligation to keep them. The promise

---

* In their answer at the Savoy Conference (A.D. 1661) the Bishops say: "The Catechism is not intended as a whole body of divinity, but as a comprehension of the Articles of Faith, and other doctrines most necessary to salvation." Bishop Ken writes, "The doctrine delivered in the Catechism is as proper for the study, and necessary for the salvation, of a great doctor as of a weak Christian or young child."

† The Parson Catechising in George Herbert's "Country Parson" (Chap. XXI.), is well worthy of careful attention.

of faith is further explained by the insertion of the Creed, and a summary of its teaching; and the promise of obedience by the rehearsal of the Ten Commandments, and by an explanation of their requirements in "My duty towards God," and "My duty towards my neighbour." The subject of prayer, as the way in which we must seek the help of God to enable us to keep these promises, is then introduced by the Lord's Prayer and an exposition of its meaning. Lastly, the "Sacraments," as "means of grace" through which that help is given, are explained.

The Catechism may therefore be divided into five principal parts:—

I. The Christian Covenant, its privileges and duties, with a short account of the first promise, of Repentance, or what we are bound to renounce.

II. The second promise, of Faith. The Creed, or what we are bound to believe.

III. The third promise, of Obedience. The Ten Commandments, or what we are bound to do.

IV. Prayer. The Lord's Prayer, or how we are to seek grace.

V. The Sacraments. Baptism and the Lord's Supper, or the means by which we may look to receive grace.

SCHEME OF THE CHURCH CATECHISM.

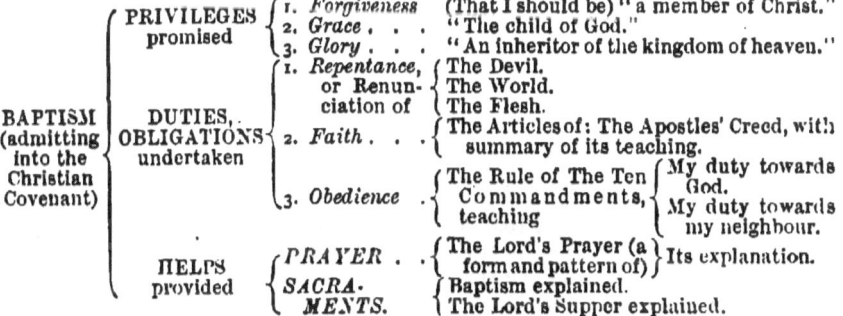

PART I.

THE CHRISTIAN COVENANT.

The Catechism begins with what may seem at first the *strange* question, "What is your name?" This is designed to make the child think of himself personally, and of his Baptism when he received that name; and to remind him that it witnesses to his profession as a Christian—that it is the name of "a soldier and servant of Christ." It is intended to bring home to him his own individual responsibility.

This name ("N or M"*) is therefore called our "Christian name," as the other name we bear, derived from our parents, is called our "surname," or additional name. (See Isa. xliv. 5; St. Mark iii. 16, 17.)

"This name was given to me by my godfathers and godmothers in my Baptism" (it is to them the words are addressed, "Name this child"), "wherein I was made a member of Christ, the child of God, and an inheritor of the kingdom of heaven."

Baptism is the instrument, or means, of admission into the Church of Christ, or, in other words, into participation in the benefits and blessings of the Christian Covenant.

In like manner circumcision was the appointed mode of admission into Covenant with God under the old dispensation. This was administered to infants (Gen. xvii. 7-10; Lev. xii. 3), and a name was given at its administration (Gen. xxi. 3, 4; St. Luke i. 59, 60, ii. 21). That Covenant was intended to prepare the way for the new and better Covenant which God has made in Christ, not with one nation only, but with all mankind. (See Jer. xxxi. 31-33; Heb. viii. 7-13.)

A Covenant is an agreement between two or more persons, in which certain promises are made by the one party, subject to the fulfilment of certain conditions by the other.

---

* It has been thought that M is put for NN plural. This, however, can scarcely be the case, as M and N are used in the Marriage Service, the former for the man and the latter for the woman. We might think this the true explanation had it not been here placed first, and used alone in the Baptismal Service.

I. Christian Privileges.

The privileges of the Christian Covenant—the blessings offered and promised to us in Christ.

"In my Baptism, wherein I was made a member of Christ, the child of God, and an inheritor of the kingdom of heaven."

In the Baptismal Service the godparents are thus addressed: "Ye have prayed that our Lord Jesus Christ would vouchsafe to receive him (this child), to release him of his sins, to sanctify him with the Holy Ghost, to give him the kingdom of heaven and everlasting life. Ye have heard also that our Lord Jesus Christ *hath promised* in His Gospel to grant all these things that ye have prayed for; *which promise* He for His part will most surely keep and perform" (wherefore after *this promise made by Christ*, this infant must also faithfully, for his part, promise, &c.).

These "promises," made generally in the Gospel, "of forgiveness of sin, and of our adoption to be the sons of God by the Holy Ghost, are visibly signed and sealed by Baptism as by an instrument" (or deed), to us individually (Article XXVII.). They are "the promises of God made '*to us*' in this Sacrament." Hence we have a right to claim and take them as our own. In this sense then we may say, "In my Baptism I *was made* a member of Christ," &c.; but in the full sense of use and enjoyment of these privileges and blessings, this can only be truly said by those who live a life of faith in Christ, and so are the children of God, renewed and led by the Spirit of God (Rom. viii. 14). We may despise and forfeit our privileges. These titles then do not necessarily imply any change of heart or character in those to whom they are applied. They refer to a change of state, a condition of privilege. They mean that the blessings which belong to such as are described by these titles are theirs, if they claim and lay hold on them; and this not *because* of their faith or conduct, but because they are God's promises, sealed to them in their Baptism. If these words are taken in a higher sense, as implying a change of heart and character, they can only be affirmed in the language of charity *—that is, on the supposition

---

* "All that the minister warrantably baptizeth are sacramentally regenerate, and are, *in foro ecclesiæ*, members of Christ, children of God, and heirs of heaven."—*Baxter's Works*, vol. v. p. 46. London, 1830.

"In our Baptism we are *sacramentally* and *instrumentally* made the

of the sincerity of those who use them, and who can go on to say "Yes, verily, and by God's help so I will."

We may compare with this the language used of God's people Israel. See Exod. vi. 4, 6, 7, 8, and compare with Num. xiv. 30. So in 1 Cor. x. 1, 5, where the "all" contrasted with the "many" (ver. 5) points to privileges actually possessed yet forfeited. Verses 11, 12, show the pertinence of this to Christians.

Christian privileges may be summed up in three words :—I. Forgiveness; II. Grace; III. Glory; relating to the Past, the Present, and the Future (so in Absolution in Holy Communion).

I. **Forgiveness.**—"I was made a member of Christ." In these words God's promise to receive us and to release us of our sins is described. "The promise of forgiveness of sin is visibly signed and sealed by Baptism."

A "member" is a limb or part of the body, such as the hand or the foot (St. Matt. v. 29, 30). "A member of Christ," then, is a part of His body, that is, of His spiritual (or mystical) body, which is the Church ("members incorporate in the mystical body of Thy Son"—2nd Prayer in Post-Communion Office).

"As the body is one, and hath many members, and all the members of that one body, being many, are one body, so also is Christ. Now ye are the body of Christ and members in particular" ("severally members thereof," R.V.) (1 Cor. xii. 12, 27).

"We are members of His body, of His flesh, and of His bones" (Eph. v. 30). "The Church, which is His body" (Eph. i. 22, 23).

This union with Christ is described under other figures: by Himself as the union between the branches and the vine (St. John xv. 1-9); and

---

children of God; and really and truly when we are baptized with the Holy Ghost."—*Meyer's Catechism* (published, as Dr. Mozley remarks, "under Laud's primacy, and a book of some authority").

"In this *lower external* and *ecclesiastical* sense, therefore, we may affirm *unconditionally* the regeneration of all to whom baptism is rightly administered. But in the *higher* and *spiritual* sense of the term we can predicate regeneration of baptized persons only *hypothetically*, namely, upon the supposition, in the case of adults, of their sincerity, and in the case of infants, of their possessing that disposition which shall lead them, when they become capable of it, to keep their baptismal vows."—*Scott's Inquiry into the Effect of Baptism*, p. 103. London. See also Bishop Harold Brown on Article XXVII., and Bishop Nicholson's Exposition, p. 14. Parker, Oxford, 1844.

by His Apostles as that of stones in a building (Eph. ii. 19-22; 1 St. Peter ii. 5, 6. See also Rom. xi. 16-24).

Baptism is the appointed means of admission into the body or Church of Christ. "They that receive Baptism rightly are grafted into the Church" (Art. XXVII.). "This child is regenerated and grafted into the body of Christ's Church."—*Infant Baptism.*

"By one Spirit are we all baptized into one body" (1 Cor. xii. 13).
"As many of you as have been baptized into Christ have put on Christ" (Gal. iii. 27).

The great gift which we receive through membership of Christ is forgiveness. "Who hast vouchsafed to regenerate these thy servants by water and the Holy Ghost, and hast given unto them forgiveness of all their sins."—*Prayer in Order of Confirmation.*

"He hath made us accepted in the beloved (Son), *in whom* we have redemption through His blood, the forgiveness of sins" (Eph. i. 6, 7).
"Repent and be baptized . . . in the name of Jesus Christ, for the remission of sins" (Acts ii. 38).

In order that this union may be a living one, we must be united to Christ by faith, so as to "live by the faith of the Son of God;" to live in Christ and Christ in us (Gal. ii. 20). This is the work of the Holy Spirit. This life will always be manifested by fruitfulness or holiness (St. John xv. 5). It is because of this oneness with Christ that, being "found in Him" (Phil. iii. 9), we are accepted as righteous for Christ's sake. Thus we become partakers of the benefit of Christ's redeeming work.

Our Lord teaches that there are branches *in Him* which do not bear fruit and are cast away (St. John xv. 2, 6).

II. **Grace.**—"I was made . . . the child of God." By nature *a* son of God ("for we are His offspring," Acts xvii. 28), I was made, by adoption into His family and household, *the* child of God, as being a member of Christ. "Being by nature born in sin and the children of wrath, we are hereby made *the children of grace*" (or of God's favour). (Church Catechism, "The Sacraments," Q. 5, p. 75.)

"The promise . . . of our adoption to be the sons of God by the Holy Ghost is visibly signed and sealed by Baptism" (Art. XXVII.).

"Ye are all the children of God by faith in Christ Jesus. For as many of you as have been baptized into Christ have put on Christ" (Gal. iii. 26, 27).

"As many as received Him, to them gave He the right to become children of God, even to them that believe on His name" (St. John i. 12, R.V.).

"God sent forth His Son, made of a woman, made under the law, to redeem them that were under the law, that we might receive the adoption of sons" (Gal. iv. 4, 5).

If we would learn what the true child of God must be and do, we should read 2 Cor. vi. 17, 18; Rom. viii. 14.

A "son" may be a prodigal, a lost son, a dead son (St. Luke xv.; Isa. i. 2).

The privileges which this relationship ensures are reconciliation (2 Cor. v. 18, 19); love (St. John xiv. 23); provision (St. Matt. vi. 26); the help of the Holy Spirit (St. Luke xi. 13); fatherly chastisement when needed (Heb. xii. 5).

The duties which it demands are the filial or child-like ones of love (1 St. John iv. 19); honour (Mal. i. 6); obedience (St. Luke ii. 49); trust (St. Matt. vi. 31, 32); submission (Heb. xii. 9); imitation (St. Matt. v. 45-48).

III. **Glory.**—"I was made . . . an inheritor of the kingdom of heaven." An "inheritor" is one who has a title to and a present possession in, and who will hereafter come into full enjoyment of, an estate.

"And he (the Lord) said unto him (Abram), I am the Lord that brought thee out of Ur of the Chaldees, to give thee this land to inherit it" (Gen. xv. 7). "I will give it (the land) to you for an heritage" (Exod. vi. 8).

Christians are said to be "begotten again" . . . "to *an inheritance* incorruptible and undefiled, and that fadeth not away, reserved in heaven for you" (1 St. Peter i. 3, 4).

The word seems to be used here in the sense of "heir."*
The kingdom of heaven may signify the Church on earth. Admission, however, to its membership is the first privilege; while this third privilege is always connected with the future, as in the following passages from the Baptismal Service :—

"That he will make him partaker of everlasting life."

"To give him the kingdom of heaven and everlasting life."

"That he may be made an *heir* of everlasting salvation."

---

* The ministers at the Savoy Conference suggested "the heirs" (rather than "inheritors"), to which the Bishops answered that "heirs" or "inheritors" is all one, quoting Rom. viii. 17.

"That finally, with the residue of Thy Holy Church, he *may be an inheritor* of Thine everlasting kingdom."—See also Col. iii. 24.

This privilege belongs to all "the children of God;" they are "heirs of God and joint-heirs with Christ."

"If children, then heirs; heirs of God and joint-heirs with Christ" (Rom. viii. 17).

"If a son, then an heir of God through Christ" (Gal. iv. 7).

"It is your Father's good pleasure to give you the kingdom" (St. Luke xii. 32).

And it is again connected with Baptism.

"According to His mercy He saved us, by the washing ('laver,' R.V. margin) of regeneration and renewing of the Holy Ghost . . . that being justified by His grace, we should be made heirs according to the hope of eternal life" (Titus iii. 5-8).

See also Heb. ix. 16; Gal. iii. 26, 27, 29.

The inheritor must not, however, like Esau, despise his birth-right (Heb. xii. 16, 17); or like the Israelites in the case of Canaan, "come short through unbelief" (Heb. iii. 18, 19, iv. 1). Compare with these Exod. vi. 4, 8; Num. xiv. 30. "The children of the kingdom" may be cast out (St. Matt. viii. 12). We must give diligence to "make our calling and election sure" (2 St. Peter i. 10, 11).

II. CHRISTIAN (OBLIGATIONS) DUTIES.

Q. What did your godfathers and godmothers then (at that time) (do) for you?

A. They did promise and vow three things in my name. First, that I should renounce the devil and all his works, the pomps and vanity of this wicked world, and all the sinful lusts of the flesh. Secondly, that I should believe all the Articles of the Christian Faith. And thirdly, that I should keep God's holy will and commandments, and walk in the same all the days of my life.

The three things which your godfathers and godmothers did promise and vow in your name—I. Repentance; II. Faith; III. Obedience.

Remember always that the promises and privileges and blessings come first. We do not repent and believe and obey in order to earn or deserve these, which are God's free gifts, but in order to receive and enjoy them. So St. Paul writes (2 Cor. vi. 17, 18, vii. 1), "Come out from among them, and be ye separate, saith the Lord, and touch not the unclean thing; and I will receive you, and will be a Father unto you, and ye shall be my sons and daughters, saith the Lord Almighty." *Having, therefore, these promises*, dearly beloved, *let us* cleanse ourselves from all filthiness of the flesh and spirit, perfecting holiness in the fear of God." Here we have the Christian privileges of acceptance and adoption promised, and on the strength of these promises the Christian duties of repentance ("let us cleanse ourselves," "come out from among them"), faith ("in the fear of God"), and obedience ("perfecting holiness") enforced.

Compare the petition of the Collect of 14th Sunday after Trinity, "*that we may obtain* that which Thou dost promise, make us to love that which Thou dost command."

I. **Repentance**, "whereby they forsake sin," is the description in the latter part of the Catechism of this first promise, "That I should renounce the devil and all his works, the pomps and vanity of this wicked world, and all the sinful lusts of the flesh." In the Baptismal Service the duty of the child is thus expressed: "To fight manfully under His (Christ's) banner against sin, the world, and the devil."

Repentance or forsaking of sin is necessary to salvation, and is therefore required of persons to be baptized.

"Let the wicked *forsake* his way, and the unrighteous man his thoughts; and let him return unto the Lord, and He will have mercy upon him; and to our God, for He will abundantly pardon" (Isa. lv. 7).

"Repent and be baptized . . . in the name of Jesus Christ, for the remission of sins" (Acts iii. 38).

Sin is the transgression of God's law (1 St. John iii. 4). It is the following and being led by the enemies or rivals of God. They tempt us to sin. Therefore we are called to renounce them.

To "renounce" means to disown (any one) as a master, to reject his claim on our service, and to refuse to "follow or be led by" him. "Dost thou renounce, &c. . . . so that thou wilt *not follow nor be led by* them?" (first question to sponsors in Bapt. Ser.).

Our Lord, in His temptation, renounced the devil when He replied to his invitation to worship him, "Get thee behind Me, Satan: for it is written, Thou shalt worship the Lord thy God, and Him only shalt thou serve" (St. Luke iv. 8). Here we see that renunciation is required by, as it springs from, allegiance and fidelity to Christ, for "No man can serve two masters" (St. Matt. vi. 24).

We here promise to follow no other Master or Leader but the Lord Jesus, into whose name and service we are baptized, or, in other words, to forsake sin—the evil ways into which other masters would lead us.

A simple illustration may help us to understand the meaning of this obligation, and to see how repentance, faith, and obedience are related to one another, and together constitute (or make up) allegiance and fidelity to Christ.

Suppose that you were lost on some wide moor or pathless plain, and could not find your way home, and that one or more persons came and offered to guide you, and show you the road, if you would follow them. If these wanted you to go in different directions, you could not go with all of them. You must make up your mind which of them you would follow, and this would be the one whom you could best trust. Thus trust (or faith) in the guide you choose would really come first. Then would come the resolve not to follow or be led by the other guides, but to follow him alone (renunciation); and then the readiness to submit yourself to his guidance, and do what he bids you (obedience). But suppose that these other would-be guides whom you have refused to follow, and who only wanted to enslave, or rob, or kill you, should try to hinder you by persuasion, or bribery, or fear, or force from following your chosen guide, then you would have to resist and struggle against them; and if they should prove more than a match for you, and you were in danger of being overcome and led away by them, you would have to ask your guide to come and help you, and enable you to defeat their designs.

Such are the circumstances of the young disciple of the Lord Jesus. He needs a guide through this world to happiness and heaven. The devil, and the world, and the flesh come to him, and offer to show him the way, if he will follow them. God also calls to him, "Wilt thou not from this time cry unto Me, My Father, Thou art the guide of my youth?" (Jer. iii. 4). In choosing Him as his Master, he must first *believe* in Him, and in His claim upon his trust and obedience, and yield himself to His guidance (this is faith). In doing this, he must resolve "not to follow nor be led by" any other guide, the devil, or the world, or the flesh, who would lead him by another way, and in a different direction (this is renunciation). He must further be ready and willing to follow His example, and walk in His way, and submit to His commands (this is obedience).

But the Christian's renunciation means more than merely saying "No." The world and the flesh and the devil are his enemies. They will try to tempt him to go back, or turn aside from following Christ, by persuasion, or flattery, or ridicule, or persecution. And they will succeed in this, unless he struggle against and resist them. And to this he was pledged in his Baptism. He was signed with "the sign of the cross," "in token that hereafter he should not be ashamed to confess the faith of Christ crucified (his allegiance to Him), and manfully to fight under His banner against sin, the world, and the devil"—the three enemies—the three false guides, whom he has promised not to follow. Thus the promise to "renounce" means an undertaking to resist and *fight*—"to be Christ's faithful *soldier*, as well as servant, unto his life's end."

These enemies are, however, too many and too strong for him to overcome them in his own strength. He needs, therefore, to call upon God for help—that is, he must pray for *grace*, for strength to be made perfect in his weakness. Hence we learn our need of prayer in order that we may keep our promises; and so prayer finds its place in the Catechism. And the help which we need is generally given through the Sacraments and other "means of grace." And therefore the Catechism has something to teach us about these also.

The three enemies of our souls, or rivals of God, or tempters to sin, are: 1. The devil; 2. The world; 3. The flesh.

1. **The Devil.**—He is, we are told in the Bible, a spirit—a fallen angel—who rebelled, with others called "his angels," against God through pride (as 1 Tim. iii. 6 seems to teach), and was therefore cast down to hell (see 2 St. Peter ii. 4; St. Jude 6; St. Matt. xxv. 41). He is called our "adversary, who, as a roaring lion, walketh about seeking whom he may devour" (1 St. Peter v. 8). This he does by trying to lead us into sin, as he did Eve (Gen. iii.), and Job (Job i.), and St. Peter (St. Luke xxii. 31), and Judas (St. Luke xxii. 3), and Ananias (Acts v. 3), and our Lord (St. Matt. iv. 1-11). He is therefore called "the tempter." He is also called the accuser or slanderer, as the word devil means; because he accuses, or gives a false character of, God to man, as in his words to Eve (Gen. iii. 4, 5), and of man to God (Job i. 9-12; Zech. iii. 1; Rev. xii. 10).

"The works of the devil." All sins are the works of the devil.

"He that committeth sin is of the devil; for the devil sinneth from the beginning. For this purpose the Son of God was manifested, that He might destroy *the works of the devil*" (1 St. John iii. 8).

In the address to the sponsors in the Baptismal Service, "the devil and all his works" includes "the pomps and vanity of this wicked world," and "the sinful lusts of the flesh."

"Inasmuch as this child hath promised by you, his sureties, to renounce the devil and all his works, to believe in God, and to serve Him."

There are, however, some sins to which he tempts *through* or by means of the world, or through the flesh, using these as baits;

and others to which he tempts us *directly*. These are such sins as have to do with the spiritual part of our nature—sins of the mind; and these are here distinguished as "the works of the devil."

We may illustrate the nature of the three classes into which all sins are here divided. If we had no bodies, we should be exposed to no temptation to intemperance, or impurity, or sloth. These are therefore "sins of the flesh." If we lived in a desert island, far from the men and things of the world, we should have no temptation to love of dress and display, or love of money. These are therefore sins of the world. But we should still be exposed to temptation, to unbelief, and pride, and hatred; and such as these sins are "the works of the devil." The temptation to these comes not through desire to gratify our bodily appetites, nor yet to please or gain the applause of our fellow-men—far otherwise; but from the direct instigation and prompting of the devil.

These works of the devil are chiefly—

(1.) **Unbelief**, the root of all sin (St. John xvi. 9); the denial or forgetfulness of God's existence and presence; the entertaining of hard thoughts of God, or doubts as to His truth, and wisdom, and love. (See Gen. iii. 3, 5; 2 Cor. iv. 4.)

(2.) **Pride.**—Entertaining high thoughts of ourselves, self-sufficiency, ambition, selfishness (1 Tim. iii. 6).

(3.) **Hatred.**—Entertaining unkind thoughts of others, envy, discontent, malice, leading to murder (St. James iii. 14, 15; 1 St. John iii. 10, 12; St. John viii. 44).

(4.) **Lying and Hypocrisy.**—Falsehood in word or act (St. John viii. 44; Acts v. 1-4).

(5.) **Temptation of others**, or doing Satan's work for him (Gen. iii. 6; St. Matt. xvi. 22, 23, xviii. 6; Rom. i. 32).

Our duty, as baptized soldiers of Christ, is to "fight manfully against the devil" (1 St. Peter v. 9), to exercise sobriety and vigilance (ver. 8), as conscious of his power and subtlety (Eph. vi. 11, 12), and "not ignorant of his devices" (2 Cor. ii. 11); and above all, to be steadfast in the faith (1 St. Peter v. 9). Eve fell because she was not steadfast in the faith. Jesus overcame because He *was*. "It is written"—God has said it—was His reply to Satan. We must fight under Christ's banner, in His strength (1 St. John iii. 8), and following His example, taking the spiritual armour which God has provided for us (Eph. vi. 10-18). If we thus fight, victory is promised to us (St. James iv. 7; Rom. xvi. 20).

2. **The World.**—"The pomps and vanity of this wicked world." By "the world" is not meant the material world in

itself, the things which we see around us, but all that in these has a tendency to lead us into sin, or to draw us away from following Christ. The world is called "wicked" (and "evil," Gal. i. 4), because (we are told) "the whole world lieth in wickedness," or "in the evil one" (1 St. John v. 19, R.V.), for Satan is "the god of this world" (2 Cor. iv. 4), "the prince of this world" (St. John xii. 31); and therefore that "all that is in the world, the lust of the flesh, and the lust of the eyes, and the pride of life, is not of the Father, but is of the world." Hence, "if any man love the world, the love of the Father is not in him" (1 St. John ii. 15, 16), for "the friendship of the world is enmity with God" (St. James iv. 4).—See also Rom. i. 25; Eph. ii. 2; 2 Tim. iv. 10.

Pomps.—"Pomp," literally a procession, means an occasion of display, outward show, pride. "Vanity," emptiness, unreality (1 Sam. xii. 21). In the Baptismal Service for "pomps and vanity" we have "the vain pomp and glory of the world, with all covetous desires of the same," which gives the true meaning. What the world offers makes a grand show, but it is unreal, unsatisfying, uncertain in its possession, and soon passes away.

"Man walketh in a vain shadow, and disquieteth himself in vain: he heapeth up riches, and cannot tell who shall gather them" (Ps. xxxix. 7. P.B.V.).

"Be not thou afraid, though one be made rich, or if *the glory* of his house be increased; for he shall carry nothing away with him when he dieth, neither shall his *pomp* follow him" (Ps. xlix. 16, 17, P.B.V.). See also St. Matt. iv. 8, vi. 19; St. Luke xii. 20.

For as what is forbidden is "the pride of life," love of display, ambition, vanity, frivolity, undue love of pleasure and amusement, desire for admiration, and greed for gain, love of money and earthly possessions.

Our "world" is made up of the persons and things which are around us, and with which we have to do.

(1.) Sometimes "the world" means the people of the world, as in St. John xv. 19. These are described in Ps. xvii. 14 as those "which have their portion in this life;" and in Phil. iii. 19 as those "who mind earthly things" (in contrast with Christians, described in ver. 20). The "world" in this sense tempts us through the influence of companionship, and society with its example, and fashions and ways; and we must not follow nor be led by it.

The people of the world tempt us to sin by—

(*a.*) Persuasion (Prov. i. 10-16) ; (*b.*) by their praise and blame, by flattery and ridicule, through love of popularity and fear to appear to be singular (St. John xii. 42, 43, v. 44 ; Gal. i. 10) ; (*c.*) by persecution (St. Matt. xiii. 21 ; Isa. li. 12, 13) ; (*d.*) by example and fashion, "everybody does it" (Exod. xxiii. 2 ; St. Matt. vii. 13).

Our duty as Christians with reference to the people of the world is set before us in Psalm i. 1, 2 ; Rom. xii. 2 ; 2 Cor. vi. 17 ; 1 St. Peter ii. 9. We are to be *in* the world but not *of* the world (St. John xvii. 15, 16). We must always remember the Lord's words, St. Matt. x. 28, 32, 33, and St. Luke xiv. 26.

(2.) Sometimes "the world" means things around us (1 John ii. 15-17) ; "the things seen," as opposed to the things not seen (2 Cor. iv. 18) ; the things perceived by sense, as opposed to those perceived by faith (Heb. xi. 1) ; the things of time, as opposed to the things of eternity (2 Cor. iv. 18). These may be distinguished as—

(*a.*) **Cares.** Anxiety about the necessaries of life, or getting on in the world (St. Matt. xiii. 22 ; St. Luke xxi. 34, x. 41, 42).

(*b.*) **Riches,** possessions, treasures upon earth (Eccles. v. 13 ; St. Mark x. 23 ; 1 Tim. vi. 9, 10 ; St. Matt. xix. 22).

(*c.*) **Pleasures** of this life (St. Luke viii. 14 ; 1 Tim. v. 6).

These, even when not sinful in themselves, or sinfully pursued, have a tendency to occupy the thoughts and engross the heart, and to lead us to make light of Christ and neglect salvation, as is shown in the parable of the Great Supper (St. Luke xiv. 16-21), or to draw us away from following Him faithfully and fully, as is seen in the parable of the Sower (St. Luke viii. 14).

Our duty with regard to these is taught us in 1 Cor. vii. 31 ; 1 St. John ii. 15 ; Phil. iv. 6 ; St. Matt. vi. 33, 34 ; 1 Tim. vi. 6-9, 17-20 ; Eccles. xi. 9, 10, xii. 1.

We must always remember our Lord's question, "What is a man profited, if he shall gain the whole world, and lose his own soul? or what shall a man give in exchange for his soul?" (St. Matt. xvi. 26).

The secret of victory over the world, as over the devil, is faith (1 St. John v. 4, 5 ; Gal. i. 4).

3. **The Flesh.** "And all the sinful lusts of the flesh."

By the flesh is meant "self,"—the traitor within which disposes us to listen to the devil and to love the world, and without whose aid these would have no power to tempt us. Sometimes the flesh is used to signify our fallen nature, with which we were born into the world, with its dispositions and desires and tempers, which are evil, and lead into sin, and even in a true Christian are contrary to, and war against, the leadings of the Spirit of God and the desires of the renewed heart. (See Art. IX.)*

As used here, however, to designate a particular class of sins, "the flesh" denotes the body, and "the lusts (or desires) of the flesh" are our bodily appetites, the unlawful or undue gratification of which is "sinful," though the appetites themselves have been implanted in us for our good. In the Baptismal Service they are spoken of as the *carnal* desires of the flesh : "These are the sins which are forbidden by the Seventh Commandment, such as intemperance in eating and drinking (Rom. xiii. 13 ; Eph. v. 18), impurity (St. Matt. v. 8, 28), sloth (Prov. xix. 15 ; Rom. xii. 11.) (See p. 52.)

We are to refuse to follow or be led by these appetites, to let them be our masters (Rom. vi. 12, 13 ; 1 St. Peter ii. 11). We are not to live for the body (Rom. xiii. 14). We must keep it in subjection (1 Cor. ix. 27). And in order to this we must yield our bodies to God, and keep and use them for God (Rom. vi. 13, 19, xii. 1 ; 1 Cor. vi. 19, 20).

Against these three great enemies we are pledged to "fight manfully under Christ's banner," and in His strength promised to be made perfect in our weakness (2 Cor. xii. 9); like David going against Goliath "in the name of the Lord" (1 Sam. xvii. 45-48). "Fight the good fight of faith, lay hold on eternal life, whereunto thou art also called, and hast professed a good profession" (1 Tim. vi. 12). Unless we do this, these enemies will overcome and destroy us ; and let us remember that all that we are called to renounce is not only inconsistent with our profession and with the service of Christ, but is also injurious to ourselves. It is from the paths of sin, which lead to misery and ruin and eternal death, Christ calls us to follow Him in "ways of pleasantness" and "paths of peace" to obtain eternal life.

---

* Rom. viii. 5-9; Gal. v. 19-22; Rom. vii. 18; Eph. ii. 3; Gen. vi. 5; St. Matt. xv. 19; St. James i. 14, 15; Gal. v. 17; St. Matt. xvi. 24; Rom. viii. 13; Gal. v. 24.

II. **Faith.**—"Secondly, that I should believe all the Articles of the Christian Faith." "The Christian Faith" means what Christians believe, as taught in God's Word, and briefly expressed, or summed up, in the Creeds of the Church.

"*The faith* which was once delivered unto the saints" (Jude 3).
"In the latter times some shall depart from *the faith*" (1 Tim. iv. 1).
"They have erred from *the faith*" (1 Tim. vi. 10).

"Articles" (literally, little joints, as of the finger) means points or facts. These are enumerated in the sentences or clauses which make up the Creed (given in the second part of the Catechism).

This second duty of the Baptismal Covenant is also described in these words:—

"To believe in God" (concluding address to sponsors in Form of Baptism of Infants).

"Constantly (to) believe God's Holy Word" (first address in Form of Baptism of Infants).

"Faith, whereby they steadfastly believe the promises of God made to them in that Sacrament" (Church Catechism, Sacraments).

It is instructive to compare these. They all mean the same thing. We believe the Articles of the Christian Faith because we believe God's Holy Word, from which they are derived, and by which they may be proved (see Art. VIII.). We believe the promises of God because they are contained in God's Word. These are the application to ourselves of the truths set forth in the Creed. We believe the Bible because we believe God, whose Word it is (2 Tim. iii. 16, 17; 2 St. Peter i. 21). We believe in God, as He has been pleased to reveal Himself to us in His Word.

Belief, or Faith, is being sure that what is told us is true. It is confidence in the Unseen, which makes it real to us (Heb. xi. 1). Here it is not merely the assent of the understanding, but such a firm persuasion of the truth of God's Word as affects the heart and will, and influences the life and conduct. Faith, or Trust in God, comes from what He has told us in the Bible about Himself (Rom. x. 17). Faith in Christ, or reliance upon Him for salvation (St. John iii. 14–17), arises from belief in the witness that God hath borne concerning His Son (1 St. John v. 10, 11, R.V.).

III. **Obedience.**—"That I should keep God's holy will and commandments, and walk in the same all the days of my life."

God's holy will means what He wishes or wills us to be and do. This is taught us in the Bible, and summed up for us in the Ten Commandments (given and explained in the third part of the Catechism). These we must "keep," that is, attend to and observe (see Ps. cxix. 33, 34), and "walk" in them (the same) all our lives. To "walk in" them is to try to obey; to aim to fulfil them; to go in the way which they mark out for us; to direct our conduct by them (St. Luke i. 6; Ps. cxix. 1, 3, 9, 35). To "walk" is also to go forward, and means here that steady perseverance in well-doing which leads to constant growth in holiness, and advance towards perfection, the aim set before us by Christ (St. Matt. v. 48).

This promise is described in the concluding address to the sponsors in the Form of Public Baptism as "to *serve* God" ("to believe in God and to serve Him").

Christian Obligation.—*Q.* "Dost thou not think that thou art bound (under obligation) to believe and to do as they (thy godfathers and godmothers) have promised for thee?" *Ans.* "Yes, verily" (truly indeed); because the promise was made *in my name*: it was *my promise* by them, and for *my benefit*: and even without that promise it would be my duty, as created by God, and redeemed by Christ, and admitted into His Church, to do this. "And by God's help so I will: and," instead of being sorry or unwilling to be so bound, "I heartily thank our Heavenly Father that He hath called me to this state of salvation through Jesus Christ our Saviour"—a state or way * of safety, if I am sincere in saying this, and am fulfilling my promises of repentance and faith † (1 Cor. xv. 1, 2); a state in which I enjoy all the means of salvation—"and I pray unto God to give me His grace that I may continue in the same (state of salvation) unto my life's end."

Our need of God's help, and hence of prayer, is brought before us more fully in the fourth part of the Catechism.

---

* So in Latin Prayer-Book of Charles II.

† "Into this state of salvation, that is, into such a state and condition of life wherein we may be saved, and shall certainly be so if he doth but perform what he promised when he was by Baptism admitted or brought into it, and what he hath now promised again. . . . But though he be now in a state of salvation, unless he continue in it he cannot be saved."—*Bishop Beveridge*, "*The Church Catechism Explained*," 1705.

PART II.

THE CHRISTIAN'S CREED OR BELIEF.

WHAT WE ARE BOUND TO BELIEVE, AND WHAT WE CHIEFLY LEARN IN IT.

Q. " Rehearse " (" repeat," " recite," Judges v. 11 ; 1 Sam. xvii. 31 ; Acts xi. 4) " the Articles of thy belief." *Ans.* " I believe in God the Father," &c.

This is called the Apostles' Creed, because it embodies the leading truths which they taught, and is the earliest of the three Creeds.* " Creed " (from its first word in Latin, *credo*, " I believe ") means a Confession of Faith—a summary of the Articles of the Christian belief. (See Acts viii. 37 ; 1 Cor. xv. 3, 4.)

We receive and believe the Creeds because "they may be proved by most certain warrants of Holy Scripture" (Art. viii.).

The Apostles' Creed consists of three parts : (1) relating to God the Father ; (2) to God the Son ; (3) to God the Holy Ghost, and contains twelve Articles or statements of truth.

PART I. (one Article).

Article I.—" I believe in God the Father Almighty, Maker of heaven and earth."

"I believe" (not *we*, as in the Lord's Prayer we say "*Our Father*," because each of us must believe and confess for himself).

" I believe " is to be understood before each separate Article of the Creed, and every part of it.

" **In God.**" To believe *in* God means more than to believe God, or that there is a God. It means to put my trust and confidence in Him as God.

---

* There are two other Creeds of the Church : the Nicene Creed, drawn up at Nicæa A.D. 325, and the latter part at Constantinople A.D. 381. This is used in the Communion Service ; and the Creed commonly called the Creed of St. Athanasius (about A.D. 430). This is used on certain days in Morning Prayer, in the place of the Apostles' Creed.

"'Ye believe in God," or "believe in God" (R.V. marg., St. John xiv. 1).
"Believe *in* the Lord your God, so shall ye be established: believe His prophets" (note the distinction), "so shall ye prosper" (2 Chron. xx. 20).
"He that cometh to God must believe that He is, and that He is a rewarder of them that diligently seek Him" (Heb. xi. 6).

"God the Father" (see p. 34).

"To us there is but one God, the Father, of whom are all things, and we in Him" (1 Cor. viii. 6).
"Grace be to you, and peace from God our Father, and from the Lord Jesus Christ. Blessed be the God and Father of our Lord Jesus Christ," &c. (Eph. i. 2, 3).
"Elect according to the foreknowledge of God the Father," &c.
"Blessed be the God and Father of our Lord Jesus Christ" (1 St. Peter i. 2, 3).

"Almighty,"—able to do all things.

"I know that Thou canst do everything" (Job xlii. 2).
"With men it is impossible, but not with God; for with God all things are possible" (St. Mark x. 27).*
"Abba, Father. All things are possible unto Thee. Take away this cup from me" (St. Mark xiv. 36).

and Ruler over all.

"The Lord hath prepared His throne in the heavens, and His kingdom ruleth over all" (Ps. ciii. 19).

"Maker of heaven and earth,"—of all things, visible and invisible (Nicene Creed).

"In the beginning God created the heaven and the earth" (Gen. i. 1).
"Thou hast created all things, and for Thy pleasure (because of Thy will, R.V.) they are, and were created" (Rev. iv. 11).
"By faith we understand that the worlds have been framed by the word of God, so that what is seen hath not been made of things which do appear" (Heb. xi. 3, R.V.).
See also Ps. xcvi. 5; Isa. xlii. 5; Acts iv. 24;* Rom. i. 20.

---

* Many of the texts adduced are selected to show the practical importance of the truths stated, as this and the following.

PART II. (six Articles).

"And in Jesus Christ, His only Son, our Lord, Who was conceived by the Holy Ghost, Born of the Virgin Mary, Suffered under Pontius Pilate, Was crucified, dead, and buried. He descended into hell ; The third day He rose again from the dead ; He ascended into heaven, And sitteth at the right hand of God the Father Almighty ; From thence He shall come to judge the quick and the dead.

Article II.—" And in Jesus Christ, His only Son, our Lord."

"The Gospel of God . . . concerning His Son Jesus Christ our Lord, which was made of the seed of David according to the flesh, and declared to be the Son of God," &c. (Rom. i. 1-5).

"And in Jesus Christ,"—*as* we believe *in* God the Father.

"Ye believe in God ; believe *also in Me*" (St. John xiv. 1).
See also St. John iii. 15, 16; Rom. x. 11.

(*a*.) **"Jesus,"** the name of the Son of God as man, given to the babe born at Bethlehem by God's command at His circumcision (St. Luke ii. 21), as our Christian names are at our Baptism. "Jesus," like the Hebrew Joshua, means a Divine Saviour.

"Thou shalt call His name Jesus, for He shall save His people from their sins" (St. Matt. i. 21 ; St. Luke i. 31).
See 1 Tim. i. 15 ; 1 John iv. 14 ; St. Matt. xviii. 11.

(*b*.) **"Christ,"** short for "the Christ," the title denoting His office. Like the Hebrew word "Messiah," it means the Anointed One.*

(The Jews believed that Jesus was the son of Mary, but not that He is the Christ who had been predicted and was expected.)
" Unto you is born this day, in the city of David, a Saviour, which is Christ the Lord" (St. Luke ii. 11).

---

* "The compound title (Jesus Christ) expresses the combination of the ideas of true humanity, and of divine office."—*Speaker's Commentary* on John xvii. 3.
"The combination does not appear till after the Resurrection, when Christ had become a proper name."—*Ibid.* on Acts ii. 38.

"We have found the Messias, which is, being interpreted, the Christ. And he brought him to Jesus" (St. John i. 41, 42).
See also St. John iv. 25, 42; St. Luke xxiii. 39.
"These (signs) are written that ye might believe that Jesus is the Christ, the Son of God," &c. (St. John xx. 31).
"The Jews had agreed already that if any man did confess that He was Christ, he should be put out of the synagogue" (St. John ix. 22). Hence Acts ix. 22, xviii. 28.

Among the Jews, Priests (Exod. xxx. 30, xxix. 29), Kings (1 Sam. xvi. 1, 13), and sometimes Prophets (1 Kings xix. 16), were divinely designated and consecrated to office by anointing. Oil was poured on their heads to signify the grace which was promised to them to enable them to fulfil the duties of the office to which they were called. Hence Saul is called "the Lord's anointed" (2 Sam. i. 14, 16). See also Lev. iv. 3; Num. iii. 3.

Jesus was "anointed" with the Holy Ghost, of which the consecrating oil was the symbol.

"Thy holy child ('servant,' R.V.), Jesus, whom Thou hast *anointed*" (Acts iv. 27).
"God *anointed* Jesus of Nazareth *with the Holy Ghost* and with power" (Acts x. 38).
"The Spirit of the Lord is upon me, because He hath anointed me" (St. Luke iv. 18, 21).

He was anointed to the three offices (which were never conjoined in any other, although Melchizedek was king and priest, and David king and prophet). He was anointed to be—

1. **Prophet or Teacher.**—"To teach men about God,"—to reveal His will. A prophet means literally one who speaks words put into his mouth by another, who is "instead of a mouth" to another. (See the remarkable illustration in Exod. iv. 15, vii. 1, 2.) Hence it is used of one who speaks God's words to men and makes known His will: "a teacher come from God:" it is only in a secondary sense used of foretelling, though it is now generally employed in this sense.

"God, who at sundry times and in divers manners *spake* in time past unto the fathers by the prophets, hath in these last days spoken unto us by His Son" (Heb. i. 1, 2).
"I have given them the words which Thou gavest me" (St. John xvii. 8).
"He hath anointed me to preach good tidings," or "the gospel," R.V., margin (St. Luke iv. 18).

"Thou hast the words of eternal life" (St. John vi. 68).
Compare St. John iv. 19, 25, 26, vi. 14; Acts iii. 22, 23.

2. **Priest.**—"To unite man with God,"—to be our Mediator; Who, after He had offered Himself as a sacrifice for sin, entered into heaven to appear in the presence of God for us, and ever liveth to make intercession for us (Heb. x. 12, ix. 24, vii. 25).

"Consider the Apostle and High Priest of our profession" (Heb. iii. 1).
"We have a Great High Priest that is passed into the heavens, Jesus, the Son of God" (Heb. iv. 14, also 15, 16; ix. 11, 12, 24-28).
"An High Priest for ever, after the order of Melchisedec" (Heb. vi. 20).

3. **King.**—"To subdue men to God,"—to rule over us by His Word, and in us by His Spirit.

"The Lord God shall give unto Him the throne of His father David, and He shall reign over the house of Jacob for ever; and of His kingdom there shall be no end" (St. Luke i. 32, 33).
"Rabbi, Thou art the Son of God; Thou art the King of Israel" (St. John i. 49).
See also St. Matt. xxvii. 11, xxviii. 18; St. John xviii. 36, 37; Rev. xvii. 14, xix. 16; 1 Cor. xv. 24-29.

(c.) "**His only Son.**" The only-begotten Son of God (Nicene Creed).

This asserts the Deity of Christ, and means that He is of one and the same nature with, and equal to, the Father (St. John x. 30, 33, 36; St. Luke xxii. 70, 71).

"And the Word was made flesh, and dwelt among us (and we beheld His glory, the glory as of the only-begotten of the Father), full of grace and truth." "No man hath seen God at any time; the only-begotten Son, which is in the bosom of the Father, He hath declared Him" (St. John i. 14, 18).
"This is My beloved Son, in whom I am well pleased" (St. Matt. iii. 17).
See also St. Matt. xvi. 16; Rom. i. 3, 4; Heb. i. 5.

(d.) "**Our Lord.**" He is "*the* Lord" (or Jehovah), because He is God.

"A Saviour, which is Christ the Lord" (St. Luke ii. 11).
"He is Lord of all" (Acts x. 36).
St. Matt. xxviii. 6, 18; 1 Cor. xv. 47; Rev. xix. 16.

He is *our* Lord. The Lord and Master of His people, whom He has purchased with His blood, and who are pledged in Baptism to His service.

"Ye call Me Master and Lord: and ye say well; for so I am" (St. John xiii. 13, 14).
"We are the Lord's. For to this end Christ both died and rose, and revived, that He might be Lord both of the dead and living" (Rom. xiv. 8, 9).
Acts xx. 28; 1 Cor. vi. 20.

Article III.—"Who was conceived by the Holy Ghost, Born of the Virgin Mary."

This Article declares His Incarnation, or taking upon Him of our flesh—becoming man. "Who for us men, and for our salvation, came down from heaven. And was incarnate by the Holy Ghost of the Virgin Mary. And was made man" (Nicene Creed).

"And the Word" (which was God, ver. 1) "was made flesh, and dwelt among us" (St. John i. 14).
"Forasmuch then as the children are partakers of flesh and blood, He also Himself likewise took part (partook) of the same," &c. (Heb. ii. 14, 16–18; Phil. ii. 6–8).
For promise of the Incarnation see Gen. iii. 15; compare Gal. iv. 4).

(*a.*) "**Conceived by the Holy Ghost.**" He had no human father.

"The Holy Ghost shall come upon thee, and the power of the Highest shall overshadow thee: therefore also that holy thing which shall be born of thee shall be called the Son of God" (St. Luke i. 35). He was therefore "without sin" (Heb. iv. 15; 1 St. John iii. 5).

(*b.*) "**Born of the Virgin Mary.**"

"Behold a virgin shall be with child, and shall bring forth a son," &c. (St. Matt. i. 23–25; (Isa. vii. 14); St. Luke ii. 7).

Article IV.—"Suffered under Pontius Pilate, was crucified, dead, and buried."

(*a.*) "**Suffered.**" This describes His whole life as "a Man of Sorrows and acquainted with grief;" but here chiefly refers to the sufferings which preceded and attended His death. (In the Nicene Creed "He suffered" comes after "was crucified.") These are called His "Passion" (Litany).

"Christ hath suffered for us in the flesh" (1 St. Peter iv. 1).
"Christ suffered for us, leaving us an example," &c. (1 St. Peter ii. 21).
"Christ also hath once suffered for sins, the just for the unjust, that He might bring us to God" (1 St. Peter iii. 18).
See also St. Matt. xvi. 21; 1 St. Peter i. 11.

"**Under Pontius Pilate.**" When he was Governor of Judæa, and by his authority. This fixes the date of the historical fact (St. Luke iii. 1; St. Matt. xxvii. 2).

"And so Pilate, willing to content the people ... delivered Jesus, when He had scourged Him, to be crucified" (St. Mark xv. 15).

(*b*.) "**Was crucified,**"—nailed to a cross of wood, and lifted up; a Roman form of punishment reserved for the worst criminals. The Jews regarded it as an accursed death. Christ had foretold that He should die this death.

"It was the third hour, and they crucified Him" (St. Mark xv. 25).
"Christ hath redeemed us from the curse of the law, being made a curse for us: for it is written, Cursed is every one that hangeth on a tree" (Gal. iii. 13).
See St. John iii. 14, xii. 32, 33; (Ps. xxii. 16; Zech. xii. 10).

(*c*.) "**Dead,**" or else the Resurrection would have been no miracle, and sin would not have been atoned for, nor death destroyed ("abolished").

"When they came to Jesus and saw that He was dead already, they brake not His legs: but one of the soldiers with a spear pierced His side" (St. John xix. 33, 34).
St. Mark xv. 44; St. Luke xxiii. 46; Rom. viii. 34; Heb. ii. 9, 14, 15; 2 Tim. i. 10; Rom. vi. 8-10.

(*d*.) "**And buried,**" to consecrate the grave, and rob it of its victory.

"And that He was buried" (1 Cor. xv. 4).
St. John xix. 40-42; 1 Cor. xv. 55; Rom. vi. 4; Col. ii. 12; (Isa. liii. 9; Hosea xiii. 14).

Article V.—"**He descended into hell; the third day He rose again from the dead.**"

(*a.*) "**He descended into hell,**"—not the place of torment, but "the unseen world," into which, when separated from the body, the soul goes; the place of departed spirits. This fact confirms the truth of our Lord's death. (See Art. III.)

"Thou wilt not leave My soul in hell, neither wilt Thou suffer Thine Holy One to see corruption" (Acts ii. 27; see also 31, quoted from Ps. xvi. 10). St. Luke xxiii. 43; Eph. iv. 9; 1 St. Peter iii. 18, 19.

(*b.*) "**The third day He rose again from the dead.**"

"And that He rose again the third day according to the Scriptures" (1 Cor. xv. 4, also 5-9).

"Him God raised up the third day, and showed Him openly" (Acts x. 40).

"This Jesus hath God raised up, whereof we all are witnesses" (Acts ii. 32).

St. Matt. xxviii. 5-8; Acts i. 22, iv. 33, xiii. 30-38; 2 Tim. ii. 8; 1 Cor. xv. 14; Rom. x. 9.

The Resurrection of our Lord proves—
1. That He is the Son of God (Rom. i. 3, 4; Acts xiii. 33; St. John xx. 28).
2. That He is what He claimed to be (St. John ii. 19-23; St. Matt. xxvii. 63, 64; St. Matt. xii. 39, 40).
3. That He has atoned for our sins (Rom. iv. 25; Acts xiii. 37, 38; Rom. viii. 34; 1 Cor. xv. 17).
4. That there will be a resurrection of the dead (1 Cor. xv. 20-24; Rom. viii. 11; 1 Thess. iv. 14).
5. That He is appointed to be our Judge (Acts xvii. 31, x. 40-43).

See also Rom. vi. 4, 5; Col. ii. 12, iii. 1.

Article VI.—"**He ascended into heaven, and sitteth at the right hand of God the Father Almighty.**"

(*a.*) "**He ascended into heaven.**" (See Art. IV.)

"And it came to pass, while He blessed them, He was parted from them and carried up into heaven" (St. Luke xxiv. 51; St. Mark xvi. 19; Acts i. 2, 9-12).

He ascended into heaven—
1. To complete His atoning sacrifice by entering with His own blood and presenting Himself for us (Heb. ix. 7, 11-15).
2. To send down the Holy Ghost (St. John xvi. 7 ; Acts ii. 33).
3. To receive gifts for men, and to bestow gifts upon men (Ps. lxviii. 18 ; Eph. iv. 8, 11-14; Acts v. 31).
4. To be our Advocate with the Father, and Intercessor (1 John ii. 1, 2 ; Rom. viii. 34 ; Heb. iv. 14-16).
5. To be our Forerunner, ascending, *as man*, into heaven (Heb. vi. 20) ; "to exalt us to the same place whither our Saviour Christ is gone before."
6. To prepare a place for us (St. John xiv. 2).
7. To reign over all things (St. Matt. xxviii. 18 ; 1 Cor. xv. 25-29 ; Eph. i. 19-23).

(*b.*) "**And sitteth at the right hand of God the Father Almighty ;**" "sitteth" denoting rest after work finished (Heb. i. 3, x. 12 ; but see Acts vii. 56, and Rev. i. 13, ii. 1). "At the right hand," —the place of honour and power.

"He was received up into heaven, and sat on the right hand of God" (St. Mark xvi. 19; Ps. cx. 1 ; St. Matt. xxii. 41-45 ; Acts ii. 34 ; Heb. i. 13 ; Rom. viii. 34; Col. iii. 1).

Article VII.—"**From thence He shall come to judge the quick and the dead.**"

(*a.*) "**From thence** (heaven) **He shall come**" (at the last day).

"This same Jesus which is taken up from you into heaven, shall so come in like manner as ye have seen Him go into heaven" (Acts i. 11, iii. 20, 21).

"Heaven, from whence also we look for the Saviour, the Lord Jesus Christ" (Phil. iii. 20; St. Matt. xxvi. 64; St. Luke xix. 12; St. John xiv. 3).

(*b.*) "**To judge the quick** (those who shall be alive at His coming) **and the dead.**"

"The Lord Jesus Christ, who shall judge the quick and the dead at His appearing and His kingdom" (2 Tim. iv. 1).
1 Cor. xv. 51, 52 ; 1 Thess. iv. 17 ; St. John v. 22, 27-30 ; Rev. xx. 12.

PART III. (five Articles).

"I believe in the Holy Ghost ; The Holy Catholic Church ; The Communion of Saints ; The Forgiveness of Sins ; The Resurrection of the Body, And the Life Everlasting.

Article VIII.—"I believe in the Holy Ghost"
(the third Person in the Trinity).

"**Ghost**" means "Spirit." He is called "**Holy** ;" because it is His particular office to sanctify or make us holy. He descended upon the disciples sent forth by Christ from the Father, forty days after His ascension, on the Day of Pentecost (our Whitsunday). (See Acts ii. 1-4.)

"And I believe in the Holy Ghost, the Lord and (the) Giver of life, who proceedeth from the Father and the Son ; who, with the Father and the Son, together is worshipped and glorified ; who spake by the prophets" (Nicene Creed).
"The Comforter, which is the Holy Ghost, whom the Father will send in My name"—"whom I will send unto you from the Father" (St. John xiv. 26, xv. 26).
"Baptizing them in the name of the Father, and of the Son, and of the Holy Ghost" (St. Matt. xxviii. 19).
"Holy men of God spake as they were moved by the Holy Ghost" (2 Peter i. 21).

Article IX.—"The Holy Catholic Church ; The Communion of Saints."

(a.) "**The Holy Catholic Church.**" The word "Church," derived from the Greek (*kuriake*), means the Lord's house : hence consecrated buildings are called "churches." In the New Testament it is represented by another word, "Ecclesia" (whence our "ecclesiastical"), an assembly called together. It means here the Body or Society which Christ founded ; the whole congregation or company of Christians, or disciples of Christ ; "all who profess and call themselves Christians" (Prayers for all Conditions of Men) ; "all they that do confess His Holy Name" (Prayer for Church Militant). The appointed means of admission into this Society is Baptism.

The Church is called "Catholic,"* or "Universal" (Litany), "throughout all the world" (Te Deum), because it is not, like the Jewish Church, the Church of one nation only (St. Matt. xxviii. 19; 1 Cor. xii. 13; Rev. v. 9); and because it holds and teaches the Catholic Faith, the form of doctrine once delivered by the Apostles to the Church (2 Tim. i. 13; Jude 3; 1 Tim. iii. 15, 16; Rom. vi. 17).

It is called "Holy" (1) because the Holy Ghost abides in it (Eph. ii. 21, 22; St. John xiv. 16); (2) because its members are called to holiness (1 Cor. i. 2; 2 Tim. i. 9; 1 Peter ii. 9); and perfect holiness will be its final state (Eph. v. 25-28). Now, indeed, and until the end of the world, the bad are mingled with the good. (See St. Matt. xiii. 24, &c., 47-51.) This, however, does not destroy its essential character. (Compare St. John xiii. 10, 11 (see note in S. C.); 1 Cor. vii. 14.)

The Church is at once visible and invisible: visible as an organised Society, having duly constituted officers and organisations; and invisible as having an invisible Head, an invisible bond of union, uniting all its true members to the Head, and invisible privileges. This latter comprehends the Church Militant here on earth, at warfare with sin and Satan; and the Church Triumphant, "those who have departed this life in God's faith and fear," and "rest from their labours."

"Upon this rock I will build My Church, and the gates of hell shall not prevail against it" (St. Matt. xvi. 18).

"Go ye and make disciples of all nations, baptizing them into the name of the Father, and of the Holy Ghost, teaching them to observe all things whatsoever I have commanded you; and, lo, I am with you alway, even unto the end of the world" (St. Matt. xxviii. 19, 20).

"Head over all things to the Church, which is His body" (Eph. i. 22, 23).

"Christ is the Head of the Church" (Eph. v. 23).

See also 1 Cor. xii. 12, 13; Eph. iv. 3-7. And for the account of its beginning, Acts ii. 41-47.

The ascended Lord carried on His work by sending the Holy Ghost; and the Holy Ghost carries on Christ's work by gathering out of the world, through the preaching of the Gospel, a people

* This title is arrogated to itself by, and sometimes thoughtlessly given to, the Church of Rome; whereas it is only a branch of the Catholic Church, and a corrupt branch. (See Article XIX.)

for His name. The day of Pentecost was the birthday of the Christian Church. Hence the connection of this Article with the preceding.

(b.) "**The Communion of Saints.**" "Saints" means holy persons. All persons are addressed by the Apostles as saints (Eph. i. 1 ; Phil. i. 1 ; Col. i. 1), because they are "called to be saints," and ought to be what the name implies (1 Cor. i. 2 ; 1 Peter i. 15).

"Communion" or "fellowship" (compare 2 Cor. xiii. 14 in the Bible and in the Prayer-Book) means having things in common—a joint participation. Christians have fellowship one with another ; with God the Father, God the Son, and God the Holy Ghost.

"That which we have seen and heard declare we unto you, that ye also may have fellowship with us ; and truly our fellowship is with the Father, and with His Son Jesus Christ."

"If we walk in the light, as He is in the light, we have fellowship one with another" (1 St. John i. 3, 7).

"The communion of the Holy Ghost be with you all" (2 Cor. xiii. 14).

"If any fellowship of the Spirit" (Phil. ii. 1).

1 Cor. i. 9; St. John xiv. 23 ; Eph. ii. 19, 20 ; 1 Cor. xii. 13-26.

They have also fellowship with angels (Heb. xii. 22, i. 14) ; with the departed in Christ (Heb. xii. 23) ; and with one another in all the ordinances, privileges, and hopes of the Gospel (Eph. iv. 3-7), and in Christian work (Phil. i. 5), and alms (2 Cor. viii. 4).

"O Almighty God, who hast knit together Thine elect in one communion and fellowship in the mystical body of Thy Son Jesus Christ our Lord : Grant us grace so to follow Thy blessed saints in all virtuous and godly living, that we may come to those unspeakable joys which Thou hast prepared for them that unfeignedly love Thee ; through Jesus Christ our Lord. Amen."—*Collect of All Saints' Day.*

This Communion is the first of the four great privileges of the Christian Church, enjoyed by all its true members—the work of the Holy Spirit. The second is—

Article X.—"**The Forgiveness of Sins.**"

Sin is the transgression of the law (1 John iii. 4). The Gospel declares that God forgives—puts away and remembers no more—sins for the sake, and through the blood, of Jesus Christ, and this *fully* (Isa. i. 18, lv. 7) and *freely* (St. Luke vii. 42-48). It is the great mission of the Christian Church to proclaim this forgiveness and its conditions. "The promise of the forgiveness of sin is visibly signed and sealed by Baptism" (Art. XXVII.). "I acknowledge one Baptism for the remission of sins" (Nicene Creed), (Acts ii. 38, xxii. 16).

The conditions upon which forgiveness is bestowed are: (a) repentance and confession (1 St. John i. 9; Prov. xxviii. 13; Ps. xxxii. 5; Acts ii. 38; Isa. lv. 7); and (b) faith (Acts xiii. 38, 39). These, therefore, are required of persons to be baptized.

"And (Jesus) said unto them, Thus it is written, and thus it behoved Christ to suffer, and to rise from the dead the third day: and that repentance and remission of sins should be preached in His name among all nations, beginning at Jerusalem" (St. Luke xxiv. 46, 47).

"Through this man is preached unto you the forgiveness of sins" (Acts xiii. 38).

"In whom we have redemption through His blood, the forgiveness of sins, according to the riches of His grace" (Eph. i. 7).

"God, for Christ's sake, hath forgiven you" (Eph. iv. 32).

Article XI.—"The Resurrection of the Body."

I believe that the body, separated in death from the soul, shall rise again from the grave, but "changed"—"a spiritual body"—made like to the body of Christ's glory, and shall live, united again to the soul, for ever.

"Marvel not at this: for the hour is coming in the which all that are in the graves shall hear His (the Son's) voice, and shall come forth; they that have done good, unto the resurrection of life; and they that have done evil, unto the resurrection of damnation" (St. John v. 28, 29).

"Since by man came death, by man came also the resurrection of the dead" (1 Cor. xv. 21; see 12-49).

"Who shall fashion anew the body of our humiliation, that it may be conformed to the body of His glory" (Phil. iii. 21, R.V.).

Acts xxiv. 15; 1 Thess. iv. 16; 2 Tim. i. 10; St. John xi. 23-27; Job xix. 25, 26).

Article XII.—"And the Life Everlasting."

"The life of the world to come" (Nicene Creed); "everlasting life after death" (Form of Public Baptism). This includes the eternal happiness of the just, and the eternal punishment of the unjust. ("And they that have done good shall go into life everlasting: and they that have done evil into everlasting fire") (Athanasian Creed).

"And many of them that sleep in the dust shall awake, some to everlasting life, and some to shame and everlasting contempt" (Dan. xii. 2).

"God so loved the world that He gave His only-begotten Son, that whosoever believeth in Him should not perish, but have everlasting life" (St. John iii. 16).

"He that soweth to the Spirit shall of the Spirit reap life everlasting" (Gal. vi. 8).

"Now, being made free from sin, and become servants to God, ye have your fruit unto holiness, and the end everlasting life. For the wages of sin is death; but the gift of God is eternal life, through Jesus Christ our Lord" (Rom. vi. 22–23).

This is, in one sense, a *present* gift. "He that believeth on the Son hath everlasting life" (St. John iii. 36).

St. John v. 24, xi. 26, xvii. 2, 3.

But as perfected in the believer's future happiness and glory, it is a future gift.

"And *the end* everlasting life" (Rom. vi. 22).

"Who will render to every man according to his deeds, to them who by patient continuance in well-doing, seek for glory and honour and immortality, eternal life." (Rom. ii. 6, 7).

"These shall go away into everlasting punishment, but the righteous into life eternal" (St. Matt. xxv. 46; 2 Thess. i. 9).

"Amen." "Verily" or "Truly." Here it means "So it is," "It is true" (Deut. xxvii. 15, &c.; Rev. i. 7). It is in this sense it is used in "The Commination." After a prayer it means "So be it."

Summary of the Teaching of the Creed.

Q. "What dost thou chiefly learn in these Articles of thy Belief?"

Ans. First, I learn to believe in God the Father, who hath made me and all the world.

Secondly, In God the Son, who hath redeemed me and all mankind.

Thirdly, In God the Holy Ghost, who sanctifieth me, and all the elect people of God.

This answer states the doctrines which are founded upon the facts contained in the Creed. It teaches us also what these facts are *to us*, what interest *we* have in them.

("God the Father made *me*, God the Son redeemed *me*, God the Holy Ghost sanctifieth *me*.")

(1.) The doctrine of the Trinity. "I learn to believe in God the Father, God the Son, and God the Holy Ghost."

"There is but one living and true God, everlasting, without body, parts, or passions; of infinite power, wisdom and goodness; the Maker and Preserver of all things, both visible and invisible, and in unity of this Godhead there be three Persons, of one substance, power, and eternity; the Father, the Son, and the Holy Ghost" (Art. I.). "The Catholic Faith is this, that we worship one God in Trinity, and Trinity in Unity; neither confounding the Persons nor dividing the substance" (Ath. Creed).

(1.) In the Bible we are taught that God, "who is a Spirit" (St. John iv. 24), is One.

"The Lord our God is one Lord" (Deut. vi. 4).
Isa. xliv. 6, 8; St. Mark xii. 29; 1 Tim. ii. 5.

(2.) The Three Persons, Father, Son, and Holy Ghost, are clearly distinguished.

"And I (Jesus) will pray the Father, and He shall give you another Comforter, that He may abide with you for ever, even the Spirit of truth" (St. John xiv. 16, also xv. 26).
St. Matt. iii. 16, 17; Rev. i. 4, 5.

And also their work in man's salvation.

"Through Him (Christ) we (both) have access by one Spirit unto the Father" (Eph. ii. 18).
1 Peter i. 2; Jude 20, 21.

(3.) The Three Persons are spoken of as on an equality, and with equal honour.

"Baptizing them into the name of the Father, and of the Son, and of the Holy Ghost" (St. Matt. xxviii. 19, also 2 Cor. xiii. 14).

(4.) The Three Persons are spoken of severally as God:—

(*a.*) The Father. "To us there is but one God, the Father" (1 Cor. viii. 6). (This is disputed by none.)
(*b.*) The Son. "The Word was God . . . and the Word was made flesh," &c. (St. John i. 1, 14).
Phil. ii. 6; Rom. ix. 5; Col. ii. 9; Heb. i.; Isa. ix. 6.
(*c.*) The Holy Ghost. "Why hath Satan filled thine heart to lie to the Holy Ghost? . . . Thou hast not lied unto men, but unto God" (Acts v. 3, 4).
St. Luke i. 35; St. Matt. xii. 31, 32; 1 Cor. iii. 16, compared with vi. 19; 2 Tim. iii. 16, compared with 2 St. Peter i. 21.

Or at greater length—

(*b.*) That Jesus Christ is God is proved—
(1.) By direct statements in the Bible (Isa. ix. 6; St. John i. 1, 2; Phil. ii. 6; Rom. ix. 5; Col. ii. 9; Heb. i.).
(2.) By His own teaching (St. John x. 30-39; St. Matt. xxvii. 63-67).
(3.) By His miracles (St. Luke v. 20-25).
(4.) By the attributes assigned to Him: *Eternity* (St. John i. 2; Ps. xlv. 6; Rev. xxii. 13, with Isa. xliv. 6), *Omniscience* (St. John x. 15; Rev. ii. 23, with Jer. xi. 20), *Omnipotence* (St. John v. 19-22), *Creation* (St. John i. 3; Col. i. 16).
(5.) By the homage paid to and accepted by Him (St. John xx. 28; St. Matt. xxviii. 17; St. Luke xxiv. 52; Heb. i. 6; Rev. v. 11-13, with xxii. 8, 9).

(*c.*) That the Holy Ghost is God is proved—
(1.) By statements in the Bible concerning Him (Acts v. 3, 4; 1 Cor. iii. 16, and vi. 19; 2 Tim. iii. 16, with 2 St. Peter i. 21; St. Matt. xii. 31).
(2.) By the attributes assigned to Him: *Eternity* (Heb. ix. 14); *Omniscience* (1 Cor. ii. 11), *Omnipotence* (St. Matt. xii. 28, &c.).

That the Holy Ghost is a Person, and not merely an influence, or quality, or gift, is proved by St. John xvi. 7, 8; Acts x. 19, 20, xiii. 2, 4; 1 Cor. xii. 8-11; Rom. viii. 26; Eph. iv. 30; in all of which places personal acts are spoken of.

(2.) The special work of each of the Three Persons in the Godhead, and their relation *to us;* what each has done or is doing for us.

I. "God the Father, (who) hath made me and all the world."

(*a.*) "Made me."

"It is He that hath made us" (Ps. c. 3, cxxxix. 14; Acts xvii. 28).

(*b.*) And continually sustains and preserves me.

"In Him we live and move, and have our being" (Acts xvii. 28; Ps. lxxi. 6, lxvi. 9; St. Matt. x. 29, 30).

(*c.*) And so loved me that He gave his Son to die for me.

St. John iii. 16; 1 St. John iv. 14.

(*d.*) And (made) all the world.

"God, that made the world, and all things therein" (Acts xvii. 24; Acts iv. 24; 1 Cor. viii. 6; Gen. i. 1).
See also under Article I. of the Creed, p. 20.

The First Person in the Trinity is called the Father, because—
(1.) He is "made of none, neither created nor begotten" (Ath. Creed).
(2.) He is "the Father of our Lord Jesus Christ" (1 St. Peter i. 3; 2 Cor. xi. 31).
(3.) He is the source of all life, the Creator of all things (1 Cor. viii. 6) and of man (Mal. ii. 10; Acts xvii. 29).
(4.) He is the Father by adoption of the members of Christ, having begotten them again by His Holy Spirit. See under "The Child of God," p. 7.

II. "God the Son, (who) hath redeemed me and all mankind."

To "redeem" means to buy back, as a pledge out of pawn, or to buy off, as a slave from captivity, with a price paid as a *ransom*. God the Son redeemed us with His own life, His precious blood, as the ransom-price.

"The man Christ Jesus, who gave Himself a ransom for all" (1 Tim. ii. 6; St. Matt. xx. 28).

Christ has redeemed us *from* condemnation (Eph. i. 7); *from* the curse of the law (Gal. iii. 13); *from* all iniquity (Titus ii. 14); *from* Satan (Heb. ii. 14, 15); *from* the world (Gal. i. 4); *from* the service and slavery of sin (Rom. vi. 18, 22; St. John viii. 34, 36), and its wages, death (Rom. vi. 23).

He has redeemed us *to* God, to serve and glorify Him (1 Cor. vi. 19, 20; 2 Cor. v. 14, 15; Rev. v. 9); *to* liberty (Gal. iv. 5; Col. i. 13, 14; Rom. viii. 21); *to* holiness (Rom. vi. 22, 23; Titus ii. 14).

The twofold end of redemption is set before us in the following passages:—

"That He would grant unto us, that we, *being delivered* out of the hand of our enemies, *might serve Him* without fear, in holiness and righteousness before Him all the days of our life" (St. Luke i. 74, 75).

"Now, being made *free* from sin, and *become servants* to God, ye have your fruit unto holiness, and the end everlasting holiness" (Rom. vi. 22).

"Who gave Himself for us, that He might redeem us *from* all iniquity, and purify *unto* Himself a people for His own possession, zealous of good works" (Titus ii. 14, R.V.)

There is no mention of redemption in the Creed, but all that it declares as to the incarnation and work of God the Son was in order to its accomplishment.

This may be illustrated by reference to the institution of redemption amongst the Jews, as described in Leviticus xxv. 25, 47, 48. There we learn that a "kinsman," or relative of a poor man, who had sold himself, or his possession, might, by paying a price, recover, in order to give back to the poor man, his liberty or his possession.

Man became poor through the Fall. He sold himself to sin and Satan. He lost eternal life (Gen. ii. 17), and became the servant of sin (Rom. vi. 17), the wages of which is death (Rom. vi. 23).

The price of his redemption and restoration must be the endurance of the curse of God's broken law (Gal. iii. 10), the payment of the penalty which his sin had incurred (Heb. ix. 22), and the rendering of perfect obedience to the requirements of the law (Gal. iii. 12; Rom. x. 5).

The Son of God, who alone was able to pay such an infinite price, in order that He might become "of kin" to us, and so have the right to be our Redeemer, took our nature upon Him (Heb. ii. 9-17), and was made man ("conceived by the Holy Ghost, born of the Virgin Mary"). He paid the ransom by laying down or giving His life (1 Tim. ii. 6; 1 St. Peter i. 18, 19) for our sins (Isa. liii. 5, 6; 1 St. Peter ii. 24; Gal. iii. 13), and by rendering perfect obedience to the law of God, "fulfilling all righteousness" (Rom. v. 18, 19; 2 Cor. v. 21), "obedient even unto death" (Phil. ii. 8). ("Suffered under Pontius Pilate, was crucified, dead, and buried, He descended into hell.")

Having thus recovered our eternal life, "He rose again from the dead" for our justification (Rom. iv. 25), and "ascended into heaven" to present the ransom (Heb. ix. 12), and sitteth at the right hand of God the Father—the evidence of its acceptance (Rom. viii. 34); ever living to bestow this recovered possession upon those who seek, and will by faith receive, it (Eph. iv. 7, 8; Rom. vi. 23); and in order to complete His work on their behalf in the redemption of their bodies (Rom. viii. 23), "shall come again to judge the quick and the dead" (Phil. iii. 20, 21; 1 St. Peter i. 5; St. Matt. xxv. 34-46).*

Christ has "redeemed me *and all mankind.*"

"He died for all" (2 Cor. v. 15).

"That He, by the grace of God, should taste death for every man" (Heb. ii. 9).

"Who gave Himself a ransom for all" (1 Tim. ii. 6; 1 St. John ii. 2; St. John iii. 16).

It is, however, only by faith that we appropriate the benefits of this redemption.

"God so loved *the world* that He gave His only-begotten Son, that *whosoever believeth in Him* should not perish, but have everlasting life" (St. John iii. 16, &c.; Rom. x. 5-11).

---

* For the working out of this illustration I am largely indebted to the late Archdeacon Norris.

III. "God the Holy Ghost (who) sanctifieth (maketh holy) me, and all the elect (chosen) people of God."

The design of redemption is that we should be holy. It is the work of the Holy Spirit to make us holy by applying to us individually the power and benefits of Christ's redeeming work through the Church; convincing of sin and revealing salvation, producing faith, which works by love and constrains to holiness or conformity to God. He puts into our minds good desires, and enables to bring the same to good effect (Phil. ii. 13).

The great instrument employed by the Holy Spirit in sanctification is the Holy Scriptures, from which all other means of grace derive their virtue (St. John xvii. 17; 2 Thess. ii. 13; St. James i. 18).

Sanctification is in this life an incomplete and progressive work, which is being carried on in the elect. Therefore we are taught to say, "Who sanctifieth," or is sanctifying, "me" (whereas we say, "God the Son *hath redeemed* me," because His work is finished and complete). We are to be day by day growing more holy (Phil. iii. 12-15; 2 St. Peter i. 5-9, iii. 18; Prov. iv. 18).

The Holy Ghost sanctifies the elect (chosen) people of God.

"God hath from the beginning chosen you to salvation through sanctification of the Spirit and belief of the truth" (2 Thess. ii. 13).

"Elect according to the foreknowledge of God the Father, through sanctification of the Spirit, unto obedience and sprinkling of the blood of Jesus Christ" (1 St. Peter i. 2).

"The elect" (St. John xv. 16-19; Acts xv. 14).

We may learn from the following passages how sanctification, springing from the love of God shed abroad in and renewing the heart, and leading to obedience in the life, is produced:—St. John xvi. 14; Rom. v. 5; 1 St. John iv. 16-19; 2 Cor. v. 14, 15; Phil. ii. 13; Gal. v. 22, 23; (St. John xvii. 17; 2 Thess. iii. 13; St. James i. 18).

PART III.

THE CHRISTIAN'S RULE OF LIFE OR SERVICE.

WHAT WE ARE BOUND TO DO.

Q. You said that your godfathers and godmothers did promise for you that you should keep God's commandments. Tell me how many there be?

A. Ten.

Q. Which be they?

A. The same which God spake in the twentieth chapter of Exodus, saying, "I am the Lord thy God, who brought thee out of the land of Egypt, out of the house of bondage."

The Commandments follow the Creed, because obedience follows and springs from faith. Duty is founded upon doctrine. If the first question of the new disciple is "Who art Thou, Lord?" the second is "What wilt Thou have me to do?" (Acts ix. 5, 6). Hence the Ten Commandments were prefaced by the declaration, "I am the Lord Thy God," &c., teaching the Israelites who the Lawgiver was, and what He had done for them, as the claim upon their obedience.

Their deliverance was a type of our redemption by Christ. That deliverance was in order that they should serve God ("Let My people go, that they may serve Me," Exod. viii. 1, iv. 22, 23). Even so our redemption by Christ is in order that we may "serve God without fear, in holiness and righteousness, before Him all the days of our life;" that, "being made free from sin, we might become servants to God" (see p. 35; Titus ii. 11, 12).*

The Commandments furnish the rule of God's service. These which contain the moral law, embodying the eternal principles of right and wrong, are binding upon Christians, and of universal and perpetual obligation.

"Although the law given from God by Moses, as touching ceremonies and rites, do not bind Christian men, nor the civil precepts thereof ought

---

* Nicholson on the Catechism, p. 79, also Nowell's Catechism, p. 23. Jacobson, p. 121 (Parker Society).

of necessity to be received in any commonwealth; yet, notwithstanding, no Christian man whatsoever is free from the obedience of the Commandments which are called moral" (Article VII.).*

See our Lord's teaching (St. Matt. v. 17-19), St. Paul's (Rom. xiii. 8-11; Eph. vi. 2), St. James's (ii. 10, 11).

We cannot, indeed, obey God's law perfectly (Rom. iii. 9, 10, 19, 20, 23; Gal. iii. 22; 1 St. John i. 8, 9), and so cannot be justified or saved by our obedience (see Deut. xxvii. 26; Gal. iii. 10; St. James ii. 10, 11; Rom. x. 5, iii. 20). We are not, therefore, under the law as a covenant of works, to obtain life by our obedience, nor, in Christ, under its condemnation and curse (Gal. iii. 13; Rom. viii. 1, x. 4).

The uses of the law under the Gospel are—

(1.) As a standard, to convince of sin—to teach us to know our sinfulness (Rom. iii. 19, 20, vii. 7).

(2.) Thus to lead to Christ for salvation and righteousness (Gal. iii. 22-25; Phil. iii. 6-10).

(3.) To be a rule of life and conduct, whereby we may give evidence of our faith and love (St. John xiv. 15; Titus ii. 11, 12; 1 Cor. ix. 21; 1 St. John v. 3).

Q. "What thinkest thou of God's law?"—*Ans.* "I think the law of God, written in two tables, to be the most perfect rule of righteousness, commanding all good things that are to be done, and forbidding the contrary." (Nowell's Second or Middle Catechism.)

In order that the Commandments may be a rule of life and conduct for us, we must regard them as only a summary of duty, the precepts of which are to be translated into principles. In their interpretation we must observe these rules:—

(1.) That the same precept which forbids the *external* act of sin forbids likewise the *inward* desires and motions of sin in the heart which would lead to those acts. Even so the precept which commands the *external* act of duty requires also the *inward* feelings and principles of which the outward act can only be the fitting expression. See our Lord's teaching (St. Matt. v. 21-29).

(2.) When anything is commanded or forbidden, all lesser things of the same nature or kind, and all like things of other kinds, as is shown in the explanation of the Fifth Commandment, are commanded or forbidden.

(3.) That the *negative* commands, which forbid to do anything, ("thou shalt not") enjoin the opposite duties; while the *positive* commands ("thou shalt," "remember," "honour"), include the

---

* The Ten Commandments alone were (1) spoken by God's voice to the people (Deut. v. 22); (2) written with the finger of God (Exod. xxxii. 16); (3) laid up in the ark (Deut. x. 2, 5).

prohibition of the contrary. Thus in each there is something required and something prohibited.

Hence the law is fulfilled by love. It is the law of love (Rom. xiii. 10). Love is the inward principle which *restrains* from wrong-doing, and *constrains* to right-doing. "Love worketh no ill to his neighbour," but also love worketh all good to his neighbour (Rom. xiii. 8, 9). If I love my neighbour, I shall not hurt or injure him, but I shall help and serve him (Gal. vi. 13, 14). Even so if I love God, I shall not do what displeases Him, but I shall try in all things to please and honour Him. The several precepts only indicate the particular ways and channels in which love should flow, the various relationships in which it should be exercised.

Therefore under the New Covenant the law is said to be written on the heart (Heb. viii. 10). It is to be observed in the *spirit* (what it means), and not in the *letter* only (what it says).

The Ten Commandments are commonly divided into two Tables (in allusion to the two tables of stone upon which God wrote them, Exod. xxxi. 18; Deut. x. 1–6). The first Table contains four, and teaches us our duty towards God; the second, six,* and teaches us our duty towards our neighbour. Both alike teach us our duty *to* God, but the first relates to the things of God, the second to the things of man.

Duty, *i.e.*, what is due or owing as a debt (Rom. xiii. 7, 8).

FIRST TABLE.—My duty towards God.

Commandment.	What I chiefly learn by it.
I. Thou shalt have none other gods but me (or no other gods before me).	1. (My duty towards God is) to believe in Him, to fear Him, and to love Him with all my heart, with all my mind, with all my soul, and with all my strength.

* So they are divided in the explanation in the Catechism, a division based upon their relation to God and our neighbour. An older and more symmetrical arrangement, countenanced by Rom. xiii. 9, allots five to each Table, the ground of distinction being that the first five relate to *filial* duties (to those over us); the second five to *fraternal* duties (towards our equals).

II. Thou shalt not make to thyself any graven image, nor the likeness of anything that is in heaven above, or in the earth beneath, or in the water under the earth. Thou shalt not bow down to them, nor worship them; for I the Lord thy God am a jealous God, and visit the sins of the fathers upon the children, unto the third and fourth generation of them that hate Me, and show mercy unto thousands in them that love Me, and keep My commandments.

III. Thou shalt not take the Name of the Lord thy God in vain: for the Lord will not hold him guiltless that taketh his name in vain.

IV. Remember that thou keep holy the Sabbath-day. Six days shalt thou labour, and do all that thou hast to do; but the seventh day is the Sabbath of the Lord thy God. In it thou shalt do no manner of work, thou, and thy son, and thy daughter, thy man-servant, and thy maid-servant, thy cattle, and the stranger that is within thy gates. For in six days the Lord made heaven and earth, the sea, and all that in them is, and rested the seventh day; wherefore the Lord blessed the seventh ("Sabbath," Exod. xx. 11) day and hallowed it.

2. To worship Him; to give Him thanks; to put my whole trust in Him; to call upon Him.

3. To honour His holy name and His Word.

4. And to serve Him truly all the days of my life.

I. **The First Commandment** teaches us the true object of worship.

1. It *forbids* us to have a false god, or more gods than the one true God.

Solomon broke this commandment (1 Kings xi. 5, 7, 8), and Ahab (1 Kings xvi. 31, 32). Heathens break it (Isa. xliv. 12-21; Ps. xcvi. 5, cxv. 4-9).

Can *we* break it? Yes! St. John writes to Christians, "Little children, keep yourselves from idols" (1 St. John v. 21). If we love or fear or obey any one or anything more than God, this is our idol, our god (we speak of "idolising" persons or things).

"No man can serve two masters. . . . Ye cannot serve God and mammon" (Syriac name for riches or gain), (St. Matt. vi. 24).

"Covetousness, which is idolatry" (Col. iii. 5; Eph. v. 5).

"These shall be lovers of their own selves . . . lovers of pleasures more than lovers of God" (2 Tim. iii. 2, 4).

"Whose god is their belly" (Phil. iii. 19).

"Who . . . worshipped and served the creature more than the Creator" (Rom. i. 25).

"If any man love the world, the love of the Father is not in him" (1 St. John ii. 15).

Riches, pleasures, self, sensual appetites, creatures, the world, are the gods of these.

2. It *commands* us to have the Lord for our God.

"O my soul, thou hast said unto the Lord, Thou art my God" (Ps. xvi. 2).

"If the Lord be God, follow Him" (1 Kings xviii. 21).

To *believe in* Him.

"Believe in God" (St. John xiv. 2, R. V.).

"The Lord He is the God" (1 Kings xviii. 39).

To *fear* Him.

"I will forewarn you whom ye shall fear: fear Him which, after He hath killed, hath power to cast into hell; yea, I say unto you, fear Him" (St. Luke xii. 5).

"Walking in the fear of the Lord" (Acts ix. 31).

"Let us have grace whereby we may serve God acceptably, with reverence and godly fear" (Heb. xii. 28; Isa. viii. 13).

And to *love* Him with all my heart, and with all my mind, with all my soul, and with all my strength.

PART III.]   *THE CHURCH CATECHISM.*   43

"Thou shalt love the Lord thy God with all thine heart, and with all thy soul, and with all thy might" (Deut. vi. 5; St. Luke x. 27).
"We love him because He first loved us" (1 St. John iv. 19).

The principle laid down in this Commandment is *singleness of heart (whole-heartedness) in God's service.*

"Unite my heart to fear Thy name" (Ps. lxxxvi. 11).

II. **The Second Commandment** teaches us the obligation, nature, and spirit of the *worship* of God.

1. It forbids false modes of worship of the true God, by making an image or likeness to bow down to or worship. The Israelites were strictly charged not to make any visible representation of God, or to worship Him under any outward form, because nothing which man can make can be like Him or represent Him truly. God is to be known and worshipped, not through the senses, but by faith. (See Deut. iv. 15-20; Isa. xl. 18; Acts xvii. 29; Rom. i. 23.)

Aaron and the Israelites broke this Commandment when they made and worshipped the golden calf (an image suggested by what they had seen in Egypt), (Exod. xxxii. 1-9). Jeroboam broke this Commandment by making and setting up two golden calves; and the Israelites by worshipping *before* the one in Dan (1 Kings xii. 26-31). These calves were intended to be visible representations of Israel's God, who brought them up out of the land of Egypt. "They made a calf in Horeb, and worshipped the molten image. *Thus* they changed *their glory into the similitude* of an ox that eateth grass" (Ps. cvi. 19, 20).

How can we break this commandment and do what it forbids?

(*a.*) By making an image of God in our minds; by unworthy conceptions of His character, thinking that He is what we would have Him or think He ought to be, rather than what He has told us in the Bible that He is (Ps. l. 21).

(*b.*) By superstition and formality in our worship, trusting in the use of forms and ceremonies, and ordinances, or postures, or words (Ps. l. 8-16; St. John iv. 21, 23, 24; St. Matt. xv. 8, vi. 7; Isa. i. 11-18).

(*c.*) By allowing any one or anything to come between our souls and God in our worship (Eph. ii. 18; Heb. iv. 15, 16, viii. 11).

2. It commands us to—

(*a.*) *Worship* God (give Divine honour to Him, to perform acts of adoration or religious service).

"O come, let us worship and fall down, and kneel before the Lord our Maker. For He is the Lord our God" (Ps. xcv. 6, 7).

"Give unto the Lord the glory due unto His name: bring an offering, and come into His courts. O worship the Lord in the beauty of holiness" (Ps. xcvi. 8, 9).

And to worship Him aright, with the understanding, and from the heart, in spirit and in truth.

"God is a Spirit, and they that worship Him must worship Him in spirit and in truth" (St. John iv. 24; 1 Cor. xiv. 15).

Through Jesus Christ (Eph. ii. 18; Heb. iv. 14-16, x. 19-23).

(*b.*) To *give Him thanks.*

"Offer unto God thanksgiving." "Whoso offereth Me thanks and praise, he honoureth Me" (Ps. l. 14, 23). "In everything give thanks" (1 Thess. v. 18; Eph. v. 20).

"By Him (Jesus Christ) let us offer the sacrifice of praise to God continually, that is, the fruit of our lips, giving thanks to His name" (Heb. xiii. 15; see also 16).

(*c.*) To *call upon Him* (in prayer).

"Call upon Me in the day of trouble" (Ps. l. 15; Jer. xxxiii. 3; Rom. x. 13).

(*d.*) To *put my whole trust* in Him.

"Offer the sacrifices of righteousness, and put your trust in the Lord" (Ps. iv. 5; Jer. xvii. 5-8).

The principle laid down in this Commandment is *spirituality in worship.*

These two Commandments *are* enforced by God's declaration that He is "a jealous God," admitting no rival (who "will not give His glory to another, neither His praise to graven images") (Isa. xlii. 8; Josh. xxiv. 19; Deut. vi. 14, 15; Prov. vi. 34).

And "visits (punishes) the sins of the fathers upon the children unto the third and fourth generation of them that hate" Him. (See, however, Ezek. xviii. 20, where we are taught that this applies only to temporal judgments.)

But "He shows mercy unto thousands (of generations) in them that (*i.e.*, in the case of those who) love Him and keep His commandments" (Exod. xxxiv. 7; Micah viii. 18).*

III. **The Third Commandment** teaches us to "give unto God the glory due unto His Name" (Ps. xxix. 2).

1. It forbids profaneness and irreverence. It declares that God will not hold him guiltless (that is, will regard him as guilty, and not overlook his sin, "will by no means clear the guilty," Exod. xxxiv. 7), "that taketh His name in vain" (*i.e.*, speaks of it or treats it lightly, thoughtlessly, or irreverently). By "the Name" of God is meant everything by which He is made known to us or which belongs to Him. It forbids—

(*a.*) False swearing or perjury, calling upon God to witness what is not true (Lev. xix. 12; Zech. v. 3, 4).

(*b.*) Blasphemy or profane swearing (the use of oaths as exclamations, or in our talk), (St. Matt. v. 33; St. James v. 12; Lev. xxiv. 11-17).

The use of oaths on some occasions is not unlawful. See Article XXXIX. (Heb. vi. 16).

(*c.*) Needless and useless appeals to God, or light use of solemn words in conversation (St. Matt. v. 34-38).

(*d.*) The making thoughtlessly, or neglect to pay vows, *e.g.*, made at Confirmation, or in sickness or danger (Eccles. v. 4, 5; Judges xi. 35; Ps. l. 14, lvi. 12, lxvi. 13, 14, cxvi. 14).

(*e.*) Irreverence or hypocrisy in worship (Eccles. v. 1, 2; St. John ii. 16; Ps. xvii. 1).

2. It commands us—

(*a.*) To honour His holy name (Ps. xxix. 2) in acts of public worship (Ps. xcvi. 8, 9, cxvi. 18, 19), and by Christian conduct in common life (1 Tim. vi. 1; Titus ii. 5; Rom. ii. 24).

(*b.*) And His Word (as the chief manifestation of that name).

"Thou hast magnified Thy word above all Thy name" (Ps. cxxxviii. 2; Isa. lxvi. 2; Ezra ix. 4; Ps. cxix. 55, 57, 72, 97, 127, 128; 2 Tim. iii. 15, 16).

(*c.*) Under God's name is included all that is said to be "called by His name," as in a special manner belonging to Him, *e.g.*, His

---

* Here, amid the stern requirements of the law, mercy is revealed, and love is shown to be the demand and the fulfilment of the law.

House, where He "records His name" (Exod. xx. 24; 2 Chron. vi. 7, xx. 9; Lev. xix. 30; St. Matt. xviii. 20). His Sacraments. His Ministers. His Day.

The principle of this Commandment is reverence for God and "the things that are God's" (holy things), (St. Matt. xxii. 21).

IV. **The Fourth Commandment** teaches us "to serve God truly all the days of my life" in worship and in work.

1. (a.) By keeping holy the Sabbath-day (day of "rest").

The observance of a stated day to be kept holy unto the Lord, and as a day of rest, is not merely a Jewish institution. It was instituted to commemorate God's rest from His creating work (Gen. ii. 2, 3; Exod. xxxi. 17). The word "remember" seems to imply that it was not newly appointed when the law was given; and we find a trace of its previous observance in the regulations respecting the gathering of the manna (Exod. xvi. 5, 23, 25, 29, 30). It "was made," our Lord says, "for man;" therefore, as Son of Man, He claimed to be its lord. The reasons, moreover, given for its observance are applicable to the whole human race. These are—

(1.) To be a memorial of creation (Gen. ii. 3; Exod. xx. 11, xxxi. 17).

(2.) To be a memorial of deliverance or redemption (Deut. v. 15).

The deliverance of the Israelites was a type of our redemption by Christ, "our Passover," which is commemorated in the change of the day of observance. (See p. 38.)

(3.) As a sign of the covenant between God and man (Exod. xxxi. 13; Ezek. xx. 12).

(4.) As an ordinance of humanity to secure rest to the labourer (Deut. v. 14).

(5.) It is also a type of the "rest (keeping of a Sabbath, margin) which remaineth for the people of God" (Heb. iv. 9).

The place that it occupies in the Decalogue proves that it was intended to be of general and perpetual obligation.

The change of day from the seventh to the first day of the week, in order to commemorate our Lord's Resurrection, whence it derives its name, "The Lord's Day" (Rev. i. 10), sanctioned, as it would appear, by Himself (St. John xx. 19, 26), and by the practice of the Apostles (Acts xx. 7; 1 Cor. xvi. 2), in no way interferes with the observance of this Commandment, which only says that after six days of labour the seventh is to be kept holy— that one day in seven is to be dedicated to the special service of God.

When it is said "the Lord blessed the Sabbath (not "seventh," as in our Prayer-Book) day," it means He appointed it to be a blessing to those who observe it. He "hallowed it," or appointed it to be kept holy.

To keep holy or sanctify the day is to devote it to God and holy uses (it is to be "holy to the Lord," Exod. xxxi. 15), especially public worship. Hence its observance is associated by God with the honour due to His house, "Ye shall keep My Sabbaths, and reverence My sanctuary; I am the Lord" (Lev. xix. 30; see also Isa. lvi. 6, 7). Our Lord's custom shows that this is the true employment of the day. "As His *custom was*, He went into the synagogue on the Sabbath-day" (St. Luke iv. 16). See also Acts xv. 21, xvi. 13, xvii. 2.

Private devotion; and the study of God's Word; and works of mercy and kindness, are ways in which we may keep the day holy.

(*b.*) By diligence in our ordinary work on the other six days of the week, and by doing whatsoever we do "unto the Lord," "to the glory of God." "Six days shalt thou labour and do all that thou hast to do" (Rom. xii. 11; 2 Thess. iii. 8-13; Eph. iv. 28).

2. It forbids all ordinary and secular work on the Sabbath-day; all secular or worldly occupations, cares, and pleasures.

"In it thou shalt do no manner of work" (Exod. xx. 10).

"If thou turn away thy foot from the Sabbath (so as not to trample upon and profane it), from doing thy pleasure on My holy day, and call the Sabbath a delight, the holy of the Lord, honourable; and shalt honour Him, not doing thine own ways, nor finding thine own pleasure, nor speaking thine own words; then shalt thou delight thyself in the Lord," &c. (Isa. lviii. 13, 14). This teaches us how God desires the day to be observed, and what He means by "keeping it holy."

Our Lord has taught us how to understand this prohibition in laying down the general principle "The Sabbath was made for man, and not man for the Sabbath" (Mark ii. 27). It was made for man's good, and not man for its observance. Whatever, therefore, is for man's real good and true welfare, that must be in accordance with the spirit and design of the institution, even though it may seem to involve disobedience to the letter of the Commandment.

Christ has taught us that it does not prohibit—

(*a*.) Works of *piety*, connected with the worship of God, and the due use and improvement of the day (St. Matt. xii. 5).

(*b*.) Works of *mercy*, and kindness towards others (St. Matt. xii. 11, 12).

(*c*.) Works of *necessity*, such as the preparation of food (St. Matt. xii. 2-5; Exod. xii. 16).

"It is lawful to do good on the Sabbath-days" (St. Matt. xii. 12, R.V.). The principle of this Commandment is the duty of the consecration of our *time* to the service of God; and to this end, of the observance of a day of weekly rest for worship and religious and spiritual refreshment, in order that we may serve God truly all the other days.

SECOND TABLE—My duty towards my neighbour is to love him as myself, and to do to all men as I would they should do unto me.

Commandment.	*What I chiefly learn by it.*
V. Honour thy father and thy mother, that thy days may be long in the land which the Lord thy God giveth thee.	5. To love, honour, and succour my father and mother. To honour and obey the Queen, and all that are put in authority under her. To submit myself to all my governors, teachers, spiritual pastors, and masters. To order myself lowly and reverently to all my betters.
VI. Thou shalt do no murder (thou shalt not kill).	6. To hurt nobody by word nor deed. To bear no malice nor hatred in my heart.
VII. Thou shalt not commit adultery.	7. To keep my body in temperance, soberness, and chastity.

VIII. Thou shalt not steal.

IX. Thou shalt not bear false witness against thy neighbour.

X. Thou shalt not covet thy neighbour's house; thou shalt not covet thy neighbour's wife, nor his servant, nor his maid, nor his ox, nor his ass, nor anything that is his.

8. To be true and just in all my dealing. To keep my hands from picking and stealing.

9. And (to keep) my tongue from evil-speaking, lying, and slandering.

10. Not to covet nor desire other men's goods; but to learn and labour truly to get mine own living, and to do my duty in that state of life unto which it shall please God to call me.

This is my duty *towards*, not *to*, my neighbour, as it is often inaccurately spoken of. It is my duty to God in the things which concern my neighbour, as the first table teaches me my duty to God in the things which pertain to God. Love to my neighbour springs from love to God, and faith in Christ.

"If a man say, I love God, and hateth his brother, he is a liar: for he that loveth not his brother whom he hath seen, how can he love God whom he hath not seen? and this commandment have we from Him, That he who loveth God love his brother also" (1 St. John iv. 20, 21).

"This is His commandment, That we should believe on the name of His Son Jesus Christ, and love one another, as He gave us commandment" (1 St. John iii. 23).

The question "Who is my neighbour?" is answered in our Lord's parable of "The Good Samaritan" (St. Luke x. 29, &c.). Every one (though a stranger or an enemy) whom it is in my power to help or to hurt is my neighbour.

My duty towards him is generally "to love him as myself" (St. Luke x. 27; St. Mark xii. 31). Love is the principle of all these six commandments; for love forbids me to do any harm or wrong, and constrains me to do all the good I can, to another.

"By love serve one another. For all the law is fulfilled in one word, even in this, Thou shalt love thy neighbour as thyself" (Gal. v. 13, 14).
See also Rom. xiii. 8-11.

The standard by which I ought to regulate my conduct is "to

do to all men as I would they should do unto me" (St. Matt. vii. 12).

This means that I am, in thought, to put myself in another's place, and to treat him as I should wish that he should treat me, if I were in his place and he in mine. (In my dealings, however, with individuals, I must have regard also to the general good, and the interests of society, *e.g.*, in giving a character, or prosecuting a criminal.)

V. **The Fifth Commandment** teaches us our duty towards our superiors, as the remaining ones teach us our duty towards our equals and all others. It is called "the first commandment with promise" (Eph. vi. 2, 3), because the promise of prosperity and long life is attached to it. It stands first in the second table, because our first duty is towards our parents and those who, as having authority given by God over us, are His representatives and vicegerents.

"Ye shall be holy: for I the Lord your God am holy. Ye shall fear every man his mother, and his father, and keep My sabbaths: I am the Lord your God" (Lev. xix. 2, 3).

1. It commands—
(*a.*) To love, honour, and succour (help, minister to the necessities and comforts of) my father and mother (Eph. vi. 1, 2; Col. iii. 20; 1 Tim. v. 4, 8). This obligation is illustrated and enforced by the example of our Lord (St. Luke ii. 51; St. John xix. 26, 27).

This is the law which creates the home, which is the foundation of society, and which establishes the discipline and subordination of life.

And because parental authority is the type and origin of all authority, and there are others who stand in somewhat the same relation to us as parents, and who also have authority over us from God, this Commandment bids us also—

(*b.*) To honour and obey the Queen, and all that are put in authority under her—that is, judges, magistrates, and officers of state (Rom. xiii. 1–8; 1 St. Peter ii. 13, 14; Titus iii. 1; 1 Tim. ii. 1, 2).

(*c.*) To submit myself to all my governors (or guardians), if my parents are absent or dead, or I am an apprentice (Gal. iv. 1, 2.)

THE CHURCH CATECHISM.

(*d.*) Teachers, if I am a scholar (Prov. v. 11–14).

(*e.*) Spiritual pastors, or shepherds, who watch for our souls, ministers of Christ (1 Cor. iv. 1; 1 Thess. v. 12, 13; Heb. xiii. 17, 18; Acts xx. 17, 28).

(*f.*) Masters, if I am a servant (Col. iii. 22; Eph. vi. 5, 6).

(*g.*) To order (conduct, behave) myself lowly (with humility) and reverently (with respect) to all my betters (superiors in age, Lev. xix. 32; 1 St. Peter v. 5, wisdom, goodness, or station and rank in life, Rom. xiii. 7). Indeed, the Bible bids me "honour all men" (1 St. Peter ii. 17).

2. It forbids disobedience, disrespect, forwardness, pertness.

The principle of this Commandment is Meekness, the temper which makes us lowly and obedient (Gal. v. 22, 23; Phil. ii. 3; St. Matt. v. 5; 1 St. Peter iii. 4; St. Matt. xi. 29).

Under this Commandment are also prescribed the relative duties of parents towards their children (Eph. vi. 4; Col. iii. 21); of those in authority in the State or the Church towards those under authority, and of superiors towards inferiors.

VI. **The Sixth Commandment** is designed to secure the rights of my neighbour's person. It is based upon the sacredness of human life. In "My duty, &c.," its requirements are thus explained: "To hurt nobody by word nor deed. To bear no malice nor hatred in my heart."

1. It forbids—

(*a.*) Murder, the wilful and unlawful taking away of the life of another. (For the sacredness of human life see Gen. ix. 6.)

The calling of a soldier is not, however, forbidden (St. Luke iii. 14). See Article XXXVII. The power of life and death is also in the hand of the civil ruler (Rom. xiii. 4), who has authority to inflict capital punishment, the appointed penalty for murder (Gen. ix. 6).

(*b.*) Suicide, or the taking of one's own life, or neglecting the means necessary for its preservation.

(*c.*) Cruelty, hurting another's body by deed, or heart and feelings by word (St. Matt. v. 22; Job v. 21; Ps. lv. 21; Prov. xii. 18).

(*d.*) Revenge (Rom. xii. 19, 17; 1 St. Peter iii. 9).

(*e.*) The feelings and tempers from which cruelty and murder arise:—*Anger* (St. Matt. v. 21, 22). *Hatred* (1 St. John iii. 15).

Malice (a spiteful desire to injure another), (Eph. iv. 31 ; 1 Cor. xiv. 20 ; Col. iii. 8). *Envy* and *Jealousy* (Gal. v. 20, 21 ; St. James iii. 14, 15).

2. It commands—

(*a.*) Kindness and help (Col. iii. 12), even to an enemy (St. Matt. v. 43-48).

(*b.*) Forgiveness of injuries (Eph. iv. 32 ; Col. iii. 13).

(*c.*) Compassion for those who are suffering or in need (1 St. Peter iii. 8, 9 ; 1 St. John iii. 17).

(*d.*) Ministration of relief to the wants of others (St. James ii. 15, 16 ; Rom. xii. 20 ; Acts ix. 36, 39).

(*e.*) Concern and provision for the spiritual need of others (St. Matt. ix. 36-38 ; Acts viii. 4, 5).

The principle of this commandment is Kindness—the manifestation of a Christian temper. It enjoins charity or Christian love.

Let us always remember the example of our Lord, "who went about doing good" (Acts x. 38) to the bodies and souls of men. We all have it in our power to do much by kind looks, and words, and acts, and by our prayers, to cheer and help and bless others; and also to do much to grieve and hurt them.

VII. The Seventh Commandment is designed to secure my neighbour's domestic rights. It has first to do with the marriage relationship between man and woman, and then generally with the keeping of the body, and the restraint of its appetites.

1. It forbids—

(*a.*) All sins against the state or institution and design of marriage, as—

Adultery, when the persons concerned are married (Heb. xiii. 4 ; Gal. v. 19).

Fornication, or whoredom, when they are unmarried (1 Cor. vi. 9, 18 ; Gal. v. 19).

Unlawful unions (St. Luke xvi. 18 ; 1 Cor. v. 1).

Polygamy, or having more than one wife (St. Matt. xix. 4-5).

(*b.*) All sins of impurity—

Unchaste acts and habits and looks (Eph. v. 3-6 ; St. Matt. v. 28 ; Job xxxi. 1), (reading improper books and looking at impure pictures).

Filthy talk (Col. iii. 8 ; Eph. iv. 29, v. 3, 4).

Impure desires or thoughts (St. Matt. v. 28, xv. 19).

(c.) All sins of excess and sensuality or immodesty, which tend to impurity—
Gluttony, excessive indulgence in eating (Jer. v. 7, 8 ; St. Luke xxi. 34).
Drunkenness (1 St. Peter iv. 3 ; 1 Cor. vi. 10 ; Eph. v. 18 ; Isa. v. 11).
Idleness and sloth (Prov. xix. 15 ; Ezek. xvi. 49).
Immodesty in behaviour or dress (1 Tim. ii. 9 ; 1 St. Peter iii. 2-5).

2. It commands to keep under the body (1 Cor. ix. 27) ; to keep it—
(a.) In *Temperance*, or self-restraint (Acts. xxiv. 25 ; Gal. v. 23 ; 1 Cor. ix. 25-27) ; moderation in eating and drinking (Rom. xiii. 13, 14 ; 1 St. Peter iv. 2-5 ; Eph. v. 18).

(b.) In *Soberness*—modesty and gravity in behaviour (1 St. Peter v. 8 ; Titus ii. 4-7. In ver. 12 it is equivalent to "temperance," as perhaps here).

(c.) In *Chastity*, or purity (St. Matt. v. 8 ; 1 Cor. vi. 15 ; 1 Thess. iv. 3-6 ; 2 Cor. vii. 1 ; 1 St. Peter ii. 11, iii. 2).

See the example of Joseph (Gen. xxxix. 7-13).

In order to this, we must yield our bodies to God, and keep and use them for God, because they are His. The body is for the Lord (1 Cor. vi. 13, 19, 20 ; Rom. vi. 19, xii. 1).

The principle of this Commandment is Purity, and in order to this, Temperance.

VIII. **The Eighth Commandment** is designed to secure the rights of my neighbour's property or goods.

1. It forbids—

(a.) Robbing—taking by force, stealing—taking by stealth, or secretly, what belongs to another (1 Cor. vi. 10 ; Eph. iv. 28).

(b.) Picking or pilfering—taking little things or parts of things, as children sometimes do of what they have been sent to buy, and as servants have it in their power to do (Titus ii. 10).

(c.) All fraud, dishonesty, and cheating (St. Mark x. 19).*
The use of false weights and measures (Lev. xix. 35, 36 ; Micah vi. 10, 11).

* Any act by which I keep back what is owing to another, or obtain anything from another without making a just and fair return, constitutes a breach of this Commandment. If, for example, I pay a shilling for twelve ounces of any article, and only receive eleven, I am defrauded or

Depreciation or exaggeration of the value of anything which we wish to buy or sell (Prov. xx. 14).

Borrowing money without intending or having a reasonable expectation of being able to repay it (Ps. xxxvii. 21).

Incurring debt beyond our means to discharge it, with all that follows (Rom. xiii. 8).

Extortion, or taking advantage of another's necessity (St. Luke iii. 12-16; 1 Cor. vi. 10).

Usury, or charging undue interest on money lent; forgery; obtaining by false pretences; gambling and betting; asking or giving unfair wages for work (St. Luke x. 7; James v. 4; Mal. iii. 5), or not rendering due service for wages received; evading payment of taxes or dues (Rom. xiii. 7).

2. It commands—

Honesty, "to be true and just in all my dealing" (Rom. xii. 17; 2 Cor. viii. 21). *Restitution* and satisfaction for things stolen or obtained by dishonest means (Exod. xxii. 1; St. Luke xix. 8). *Industry* in an honest calling, that we may not be tempted to dishonesty (1 Thess. iv. 11, 12; 2 Thess. iii. 12). *Generosity*, readiness to give to, instead of taking from, others (Eph. iv. 28; St. Luke xi. 41; 1 Tim. vi. 18).

The principle of this commandment is Honesty.

IX. **The Ninth Commandment** is designed to secure my neighbour's character and reputation. It teaches the duty of government of the tongue with reference to our fellow-men.

1. It forbids—

(*a*.) *Perjury*, or bearing false witness in a court of law (Deut. xix. 16-20). (Instances of: 1 Kings xxi. 9-14; St. Mark xiv. 56; Acts vi. 11-14, xxv. 7.)

(*b*.) All unjust and untrue accusations or charges (St. Luke iii. 14; 2 Tim. iii. 3). (Instances of: Gen. xxxix. 14; 2 Sam. xvi. 1-3, with xix. 27.)

(*c*.) *Evil-speaking*, or speaking ill of another, spreading reports to his disadvantage unnecessarily (St. James iv. 11; Titus iii. 2; Ps. xv. 1-3; Eph. iv. 31); "tale-bearing" (Lev. xix. 16).*

robbed by the seller of the penny for which I obtain nothing in return; or if I receive wages for ten hours' work, and only do as much as I could in nine hours, I am defrauding or robbing my employer of the tenth part of what he pays me.

* It may, however, be necessary and right to say what we know to another's disadvantage, as in giving a character, or a warning against

(*d.*) *Slandering*, when evil-speaking is joined with lying (Ps. xv. 3, P.B.V., ci. 5; Prov. x. 18. (Instance of: 2 Sam. xvi. 3, xix. 26, 27.)

(*e.*) *Lying*, or saying what we know to be untrue (St. John viii. 44). This is not only a great sin against God (Ps. xxxi. 5, li. 6; Lev. xix. 11; Prov. vi. 16, 17, 19, xii. 22; Rev. xxi. 8, 27, xxii. 15), but also against our neighbour, because it deceives him, and defrauds him of the truth which is his due at our hands (Eph. iv. 25 (see note in *Speaker's Commentary*); Col. iii. 9; Zech. viii. 16).

Equivocation, or using words of doubtful or double meaning; *Exaggeration*, or colouring and adding to the truth; *Diminution* or detraction, not telling the whole truth; and *Prevarication*, or evading the truth, are all forms of lying.

(*f.*) *Idle talking* (St. Matt. xii. 36; Prov. x. 19).

2. It commands us—

(*a.*) Always to speak the truth (Eph. iv. 15, 25; Ps. xv. 2; Mal. ii. 6).

(*b.*) To keep our promises (Ps. xv. 5, P.B.V.).

(*c.*) To think and speak kindly of others (1 Cor. xiii. 5, 7; Prov. xxxi. 26).

(*d.*) And therefore to keep constant watch and guard over our tongues (Ps. xxxiv. 13, xxxix. 1; St. James i. 26; 1 St. Peter iii. 10), and knowing how hard it is to rule the tongue (St. James iii. 2-9), and yet how essential it is (St. James i. 26), we have need constantly and earnestly to pray for grace to enable us to do this (Ps. cxli. 3, cxx. 2).

These are good rules to be observed—

(1.) Avoid talkativeness, because see Prov. x. 19.

(2.) Be "slow to speak." Think before you say anything (St. James i. 19).

(3.) Let "the law of kindness" be "in your tongue" (Prov. xxxi. 26).

(4.) Always remember that God hears you (Ps. cxxxix. 4).

The principle of this Commandment is Truthfulness.

him; but this should be done from a sense of duty, and for a good purpose, and not because we take pleasure, as is too frequently the case, in exposing our brother's failings and faults and falls. There is commonly much sin in gossip (1 Tim. v. 13). We ought to refuse to listen to or encourage such talking (Prov. xxv. 23), and to refrain from repeating what we do hear, and never to take pleasure in hearing or speaking ill of another.

X. **The Tenth Commandment** is unlike the others in the letter, inasmuch as it applies not to deeds and words, but to the thoughts and desires of the heart. It gives us, however, a key to the interpretation of all the rest (see Rom. vii. 7). It taught St. Paul to understand the spiritual nature of the law, and thus convinced him of sin. It serves also as a guard upon all the rest, as it forbids us to hurt our neighbour in intention, and even to desire to injure him, or do what is forbidden: for the origin of all evil is in the heart (St. Matt. xv. 19, xxiii. 25, 26; St. James i. 14, 15).

1. It forbids—

(*a*.) Generally the desire of what is wrong and forbidden— "lust" (Rom. vii. 7, R.V. margin).

(*b*.) *Covetousness.* "To covet or desire other men's goods." To covet means to desire sinfully or unlawfully (Micah ii. 2). We may wish for a thing if our neighbour is willing to part with it, and we are able to buy it. We may desire to succeed in business, or to excel, or rise in the world, if we do not do this sinfully, with discontent at our own lot, and envy at the lot of others (Ps. cxix. 36; St. Luke xii. 15; 1 Cor. vi. 10; Eph. v. 5; Col. iii. 5).

(*c*.) Especially love of money (1 Tim. vi. 9, 10; Prov. xxviii. 20).

Covetousness is the source whence all manner of sins proceed. "The love of money is a root of all kinds of evil" (1 Tim. vi. 10, R.V.).

Instances.—It led Achan into sacrilege and theft (Josh. vii. 20, 21); Gehazi into lying (2 Kings v. 20-27); Ahab (1 Kings xxi. 1-7) into breaking the Ninth Commandment (vers. 8-14), the sixth (vers. 10, 19), and the eighth (vers. 16, 19); Judas into betraying Christ (St. Matt. xxvi. 15, 16). It kept back the young ruler from following Christ (St. Matt. xix. 21-25). See also St. Matt. xiii. 22.

See Collect of St. Matthew's Day.

2. It enjoins—

(*a*.) *Contentment.* "Be ye free from the love of money: content with such things as ye have" (Heb. xiii. 5, R.V.; St. Matt. vi. 19, 25-34; 1 Tim. vi. 6-9).

Examples.—The Shunammite woman (2 Kings iv. 13); St. Paul (Phil. iv. 11).

(b.) *Industry.*—"To learn and labour truly (honestly) to get mine own living" (1 Thess. iv. 11 ; 2 Thess. iii. 12).

(c.) *Fidelity.*—"And to do my duty in that state of life unto which it shall please God to call me"—in the occupation, situation, calling, or circumstances, of prosperity or adversity in which, in God's providence, I may now, or at any future time, be placed (1 Cor. vii. 20–24).

Contented Industry is the principle of this Commandment.

Note.—This Commandment does not forbid us to seek to enrich or advance ourselves by honest and lawful means, through the exercise of our abilities, ingenuity, and industry; otherwise a valuable and necessary stimulus to enterprise would be withdrawn. It forbids us, however, to make these the great ends of life, or for these to neglect the "one thing needful." It forbids us to be anxious and troubled about them, or to be unwilling cheerfully to submit to disappointments if God so wills it. It forbids us to neglect the duties of our calling in life because it is not other than it is.

In these Commandments, then, we have given to us the Rule of—
(1.) A Godly life, I. to V.,—our duty towards God.
(2.) A Sober life, VII. and X.,—our duty towards ourselves.
(3.) A Righteous life, V. to X.,—our duty towards our neighbours.

"Teaching us that, denying ungodliness and worldly lusts, we should live soberly, righteously, and godly in this present world" (Titus ii. 12).

PART IV.

PRAYER—THE CHRISTIAN'S RESOURCE.

HOW WE ARE TO OBTAIN HELP TO KEEP OUR PROMISES.

WE have now learned what a Christian's obligations and duties are : what our godfathers and godmothers promised in our name at our Baptism, and what we assent to, and promise that we will endeavour ourselves faithfully to observe at our Confirmation. If we have thoughtfully and seriously followed what we have been taught, we must have been led to ask, "How can I do all this? How dare I undertake it?" These enemies, how shall I overcome them? These temptations, how shall I resist them? These truths, how shall I believe them? These

Commandments, how shall I keep them? We shall have been led to feel our need of help—of God's help—that is, of *grace;* and we shall be ready to ask, "Can we obtain that grace, and how? By what means can we get it?" Here, then, it is that the subject of prayer comes in. This is why it has a special place in the Catechism.

Such is the teaching of the words of the *Catechist* (not called a Question) which introduce the Lord's Prayer.

"My good child, know this, that thou art not able to do these things of thyself, nor to walk in the Commandments of God, and to serve Him, without His special grace; which thou must learn at all times to call for by diligent prayer. Let me hear, therefore, if thou canst say the Lord's Prayer."

In these words we are instructed—

(1.) That we cannot fulfil the obligations of the Christian Covenant "*of ourselves,*" by our own wisdom, and strength, and goodness (St. John xv. 5; Rom. vii. 18; 2 Cor. iii. 5; Gal. v. 17). (See also Article X., and Collect of 2nd Sunday in Lent.)

(2.) That in order to be able to fulfil them *we need the special grace of God*—that is, God's help given specially to *each of us* for *our* need (2 Cor. xii. 9; Phil. iv. 13).

(3.) That in order to obtain this grace *we must call for it by prayer* (St. Matt. vii. 7–12; St. James i. 5); and this we must *learn* or be taught how to do (St. Luke xi. 1; Rom. viii. 26).

In the answer to the question in the earlier part of the Catechism, "Dost thou not think?" &c., we are taught to say, "Yes, verily, and *by God's help* so I will . . . and *I pray unto God* to give me His grace, that I may continue in the same (state of salvation) unto my life's end." See also Preface to the Order of Confirmation.

What is Prayer? Not merely an act of worship (though it is this; see under Second Commandment (*c.*), p. 44), but it is also an asking God for what we need and want (Phil. iv. 6; St. Matt. vii. 7–12; St. Luke xi. 5–11).

In order to obtain what we ask, our prayer must be—

(*a.*) Offered *in faith, believing* (Heb. xi. 6; St. James i. 6, 7; St. Mark xi. 24).

(*b.*) Offered in the Name, and through the mediation, of Christ (St. John xvi. 23, 24, 26, xiv. 13, 14; Heb. iv. 15, 16).

(*c.*) According to and in submission to the will of God (1 St. John v. 14; St. Luke xxii. 42; St. James iv. 3).

(*d.*) From the heart, and sincere (St. Matt. vi. 7, xv. 8; Jer. xxix. 12, 13).
(*e.*) Earnest and persevering (St. James v. 16; St. Luke xi. 5-11, xviii. 1).
(*f.*) Humble (Ps. ix. 12; St. Luke xviii. 13, 14; Isa. lxvi. 2).

We need also to be taught how, and for what, we should pray; and therefore our Lord was pleased, in answer to the request of His disciples, "Lord, teach us to pray" (St. Luke xi. 1), to give to them, and to us, what we therefore call "The Lord's Prayer." This was intended to serve—

(1.) As a *Form* of Prayer to be *used* by us (like the prayers in our Book of Common Prayer), "*When* ye pray, *say*" (St. Luke xi. 2).

(2.) As a *Model* or *Pattern* of Prayer for us *to copy*—teaching us what our prayers should be like. It is as the *Pattern* Prayer it finds its place in the Catechism, "*After this manner* therefore pray ye" (St. Matt. vi. 9).

The Lord's Prayer may be divided into four parts.

I. The Invocation or Address. — "Our Father, which art in heaven."

II. The Petitions :—
   (1.) Three for God's glory.
     "Hallowed be Thy name."
     "Thy kingdom come."
     "Thy will be done in earth, as it is in heaven."

   (2.) Three (or four) for our own necessities.
     "Give us this day our daily bread."
     "And forgive us our trespasses, as we forgive them that trespass against us."
     "And lead us not into temptation."

III. The Doxology (found only in the Sermon on the Mount (St. Matt. vi. 13), and not added in the Catechism).
     "But deliver us from evil."
     "For thine is the kingdom, and the power, and the glory, for ever."

IV. The Assent.   "Amen."

Note.—In the Prayer-Book the Form with the Doxology is used in services of thanksgiving, and portions of the services which have this character. It is used without the Doxology in penitential services and portions of services.

Q. "What desirest thou of God in this prayer?"

Ans. "I desire my Lord God, our Heavenly Father, who is the giver of all goodness,

"To send His grace unto me and to all people: that we may worship Him ('as we ought to do').

("That we may) serve Him (as we ought to do).

"And obey Him as we ought to do.

"And I pray unto God that He will send us all things that be needful both for our souls and bodies.

"And that He will be merciful unto us and forgive us our sins.

"And that it will please Him to save and defend us in all dangers, ghostly and bodily.

"And that He will keep us from all sin and wickedness, and from our ghostly enemy, and from everlasting death.

"And this I trust He will do of His mercy and goodness, through our Lord Jesus Christ. And therefore I say, Amen. So be it."

"Our Father, which art in heaven."

"Hallowed be Thy name."

"Thy kingdom come."

"Thy will be done in earth, as it is in heaven."

"Give us this day our daily bread."

"And forgive us our trespasses, as we forgive them that trespass against us."

"And lead us not into temptation."

"But deliver us from evil."

"Amen."

I. Invocation.—"**Our Father**" (see under "The Child of God," p. 7, and "I believe in God the Father," pp. 20, 34). This title inspires confidence in asking (St. Matt. vii. 9–12; St. Luke xv. 18; St. Matt. vi. 26; Ps. ciii. 13; 1 St. John iii. 1).

"**Our**" reminds us of our brethren, the other children of the same Father (St. Matt. xxiii. 8, 9), and teaches us that we ought not to be selfish in our prayers ("to me and to all people").

St. Augustine calls the Lord's Prayer "the fraternal prayer."

"**Which (who) art in heaven.**" This designation reminds us—

(*a.*) That God is everywhere near to us; not in this place or that only (St. John iv. 21; Acts vii. 48-51, xvii. 27, 28).*

(*b.*) How high and great He is (Isa. lvii. 15), and therefore to be approached with *reverence* and *humility* (Eccles. v. 2; Heb. xii. 28); although through Christ we may come *boldly* (Heb. iv. 15, 16).

(*c.*) That He is *able* to do all we ask (as "Father" assures us that He is willing; Ps. xi. 4, ciii. 19).

"Who is the giver of all goodness" (*i.e.*, all that is good, see use of the word in Exod. xviii. 9; Ps. xxi. 3, cvii. 9; and in the Prayer for the Royal Family (Morning Prayer), and Nowell's Catechism (Larger), "Withdrawing of some goodness," p. 149, Parker Society edition), † (St. James i. 17).

II. **Petitions.**—Six or seven, according as we unite or separate the two last clauses (Nowell and Bishop Nicholson reckon six). These, although so few and brief, sum up all our needs.

The first three have to do with the things of God, which, according to our Lord's rule (St. Matt. vi. 33), we should "seek first." They are petitions for God's glory: the rest are for the supply of *our* wants; and yet we are to seek these chiefly in order that we may live to God's glory.

1. "**Hallowed be Thy name.**" The name of a person distinguishes him and sets him before us. The "name" of God is the revelation of Himself and of His character which He has been pleased to give to us, and everything by which He is made known to us (Exod. iii. 13, 14, xxxiv. 5-7; St. John xii. 28, xvii. 6; Ps. viii. 1, ix. 10).

"Hallowed" means treated as holy—reverenced. (In the Fourth Commandment it means set apart as holy, commanded to be kept "holy.")

In this petition, then, we pray that we and all people may feel and show due reverence for God and the things of God—"may worship Him as we ought to do" (Ps. lxxxix. 7, xcix. 3; Heb. xiii. 28).

2. "**Thy kingdom come.**" The kingdom of God or of heaven means in Scripture—

---

* See Nowell's Catechism (Larger), p. 193. Parker Society edition.

† "I charge you, as ye hope for any goodness."—Shakespeare, *Richard III.*, Act i. scene 4.

(*a.*) The Church which Christ has established upon earth (St. Matt. xiii. 41, 47; Acts i. 3). We here ask that this may be enlarged and extended over the whole world. It is therefore a missionary prayer (Ps. ii. 8, lxvii. 2; Hab. ii. 14; Rev. xi. 15).

(*b.*) The reign of Christ in the hearts and over the lives of His people (Rom. xiv. 17; St. Luke xvii. 21; St. Matt. xiii. 44-47). We pray that He may rule in us, and that we may give ourselves to His service.

(*c.*) The reign of Christ in glory, when He shall come again (St. Luke xix. 15; Rev. xii. 10). We pray that this may be hastened ("hasten Thy kingdom"—Burial Service), (Rev. xxii. 20).

If we truly desire what we ask in this petition, we shall be ready to work for its accomplishment by furthering the spread of the Gospel through our alms and prayers in aid of missionary work; by seeking through our influence, example, and efforts to bring others into the Church of Christ, and unto obedience to Him; and by diligent watchfulness and preparation for His second coming (St. Matt. xxv. 1-13). We therefore ask for grace "that we may *serve* God as we ought to do."

3. "**Thy will be done in earth, as it is in heaven.**" This will be the result of the reign of Christ in our hearts. The will of God is generally that we should be saved (1 Tim. ii. 4); that we should be holy (1 Thess. iv. 3). It is revealed to us in His Word (2 Tim. iii. 16; Rom. xii. 2), and is summed up for us, as the rule of life, in the Ten Commandments. The will of God concerning us is also manifested in His providential ordering of our circumstances.

(*a.*) We are to obey His commandments, as the holy angels do in heaven, willingly, constantly, perfectly (Ps. ciii. 20, 21; Rev. vii. 15). "They alway do God service in heaven" (Collect of St. Michael and All Angels).

(*b.*) We are to submit to and be contented with His appointments concerning us—the way of resignation under suffering (St. Luke xxii. 42; Acts xxi. 14; 1 Sam. iii. 18; Job i. 21). The will of God was the rule of the perfect life of our Lord in both senses (St. John vi. 38, iv. 34; St. Luke xxii. 42; St. John xviii. 11).

In this petition we pray that God's will may be the rule of our lives that we may *obey* Him as we ought to do." (See Collect of 1st Sunday after Epiphany, and 2nd Sunday after Easter.)

(Petitions for the supply of our own and others' needs: for Provision, Pardon, Protection, Preservation follow.)

4. **"Give us this day our daily bread."** This is a prayer for provision—

(1.) For our *bodies*. Bread stands for "all things that be needful" for them—sustenance, food, clothing, shelter. (See Gen. iii. 19, xxviii. 20; St. Luke xv. 17; 1 Tim. vi. 6–8.)

Our food is God's gift (Ps. civ. 27, 28, cxxxvi. 25); for (*a*) it is His "creature," created by Him (1 Tim. iv. 3–6). (See use of the word "creatures" of bread and wine in prayer of consecration in "The Communion"), (Ps. civ. 15, cxlv. 15, 16, lxv. 9, &c.); and (*b*) though we or our parents work to obtain it, it is God who gives us and them ability to work and to get money (Prov. x. 22; Deut. viii. 18); and (*c*) His blessing upon it alone makes our food to nourish us.

We are taught to ask for bread only, not luxuries, for "food convenient for us" (Prov. xxx. 8), and thus to be moderate in our desires and contented with what we have.

"Give us *this day* our *daily* bread," or "day by day" (St. Luke xi. 3; St. Matt. vi. 34). We ask only for to-day, and are thus taught a lesson of faith and trust. (Thus God fed the Israelites, Exod. xvi. 4, 17–27.)

While we pray God to give us our bread, we must be diligent in working for it (Prov. x. 4; 2 Thess. iii. 10–12); and while we pray God to give bread to other people, *we* must be ready to give to them of what He has given to us (St. James ii. 15, 16; 1 St. John iii. 17).

(2.) For our *souls* (Deut. viii. 3). This we should chiefly desire (St. John vi. 27). Jesus Christ is "the Bread of Life" that feeds the soul (St. John vi. 35, 53) by the operation of the Holy Spirit (St. Luke xi. 13). We should ask, "Lord, evermore give us this bread" (St. John vi. 34). The word of God, therefore, which reveals Christ, becomes food for our souls (St. Matt. iv. 4; 1 St. Peter ii. 2; Ps. xix. 7, 8; 2 Tim. iii. 16, 17; Job xxiii. 12).

The Sacrament of the Lord's Supper is a means whereby the faithful spiritually eat and drink the body and blood of Christ to the strengthening and refreshing of their souls. "God hath given His Son . . . to be our spiritual food and sustenance in that Holy Sacrament. (Exhortation giving warning of celebration of the Holy Communion.)

It is *by faith* we feed upon Christ in our hearts (St. John vi. 35).

While we pray to God to give to us and others all things that be needful for our souls, we must be *thankful* for His unspeakable gift ; *diligent* in the study of His Word and in the use of the other "means of grace," and especially Holy Communion ; *trustful* and dependent on Him alone for spiritual strength (1 St. Peter iv. 19 ; 2 Tim. i. 12), and *concerned* to promote the spiritual welfare of others, and provide the means of grace for them (Eph. iii. 14-20).

See Collect of 8th Sunday after Trinity.

5. **"And forgive us our trespasses."** If we had no sin we should only need to ask God to *give ;* as sinners, we need also *forgiveness,* without which all God's gifts cannot satisfy us, or make us happy.

In this petition we confess our sins and plead for their pardon. (In St. Luke xi. 4, it runs "forgive us our sins.") Sin is the transgression of God's law (1 St. John iii. 4) "by thought, word, or deed, by doing the things we ought not to do, or leaving undone the things we ought to do." Sins are here called "trespasses" (a word taken from St. Matt. vi. 14). "Trespass" (passing or stepping across) means going over the line which marks the right way—the way of God's commandments (Ps. cxix. 9, 10, 27, 32), and treading on forbidden ground—"going astray." "Transgression" means very much the same. (See Ps. cxix. 176 ; Isa. liii. 6 ; and the Parables in St. Luke xv.)

In St. Matt. vi. 12 the petition is, "forgive us our *debts.*" Debt is what we owe, what is *due* from us to God. We owe to Him obedience, and when we do not pay this, we incur a debt of punishment or satisfaction to God's justice—eternal death (Rom. vi. 23). "The wages of sin is death" (Ezek. xviii. 4).

Debts are compared to sins in St. Luke vii. 41-50; St. Matt. xviii. 23-35.

We pray that God will not remember our sins against us, but will put them away and blot them out ; and that He will not enter into judgment with us, and exact the penalty or demand the debt, but will restore to us His favour, and cleanse and renew us. (See Ps. li.) And this God promises in the Gospel to do for Jesus Christ's sake (St. Luke xxiv. 46, 47 ; Eph. i. 7, iv. 32 ; 1 St. John i. 9) :—a promise sealed to us by Baptism (Art. XXVII.). See on "The forgiveness of sins" in the Creed, p. 30.

"As we forgive them that trespass against us." In St. Luke xi. 4 it is "for we also forgive every one that is indebted to us." We do not here ask God to forgive us on the ground of our forgiveness of others, but, in asking forgiveness at God's hand, we express our readiness to forgive those that have offended us. See St. Mark xi. 25 ; St. Matt. v. 23, 24.

God's mercy in forgiving us is to be the motive and the measure of our forgiveness of others (Eph. iv. 32 ; Col. iii. 13 ; St. Luke vi. 36 ; St. Matt. xviii. 21, &c.). This is, therefore, made the condition on which God forgives us (St. Matt. vi. 14, 15, xviii. 35 ; St. Luke vi. 37 ; St. James ii. 13).

If, then, we do not possess and cherish a forgiving disposition, we show that we have not sought and found forgiveness ; and we ask God, when we use this petition, *not to* forgive us.

(For examples of forgiveness of others : St. Luke xxiii. 34 ; Acts vii. 60 ; 2 Tim. iv. 16.)

6. "**And lead us not into temptation.**" "Temptation" means trial to prove us and show what we are (Deut. viii. 2). Satan, "the Tempter" (St. Matt. iv. 1, 3), tempts us by trying to lead us into sin. In this sense God tempts no man (St. James i. 13, 14). In the sense, however, of bringing us into circumstances which will call forth and manifest our characters, God may "tempt" us as He did Abraham (Gen. xxii. 1, 12), and Hezekiah (2 Chron. xxxii. 31). Sometimes He permits Satan to tempt us for this purpose (Job i. 12, ii. 6). Hence Job says (xxiii. 10), "When He hath tried me, I shall come forth as gold." (Compare 1 St. Peter i. 6, 7.) Thus was our Lord tempted (St. Matt. iv. 1).

Illustration.—If a companion offered you a shilling if you would tell a lie or steal something, he would be tempting you as Satan does ; and if God gave you grace to refuse, the temptation would only serve to prove your truthfulness or honesty, and to strengthen your character. If a general were to order a young soldier to occupy a post of danger in a battle, in order to "try his mettle" and make him brave, he would be acting as God does.

When, then, we use this petition, we ask God not to suffer Satan to entice us into sin, but to strengthen us to resist him ; not to put our faith to too severe a test, but to enable us to "endure temptation" (St. James i. 12). We pray that "He will save and defend us *in*" (not necessarily *from :* St. James i. 2, 3) "all dangers *ghostly*" (spiritual, to our souls), all "which may assault and hurt the soul." See Collect of 2nd Sunday in Lent, and 3rd and 4th after Epiphany.

E

Such strength and protection is promised (2 St. Peter ii. 9; 1 Cor. x. 13; Heb. ii. 18).

If we look for this deliverance, we must be humble and conscious of our own weakness (1 Cor. x. 12). We must not run into temptation like Peter, but must watch and pray lest we enter into temptation (St. Matt. xxvi. 41). If we desire such deliverance for others, we must take heed that we do not put temptation in their way (Rom. xiv. 13).

We pray also in this petition that God "will save and defend us in all dangers bodily"—protect us from sickness and accident, and all that may hurt the body (Ps. ciii. 3, and xci. cxxi.).

7. "**But deliver us from evil.**"* Many things which we may think to be *evil*, such as losses, disappointments, sufferings, sicknesses, may be really good for us (Ps. cxix. 71); while things which we think good might be evil for us. We know, however, that *sin* is always evil—*the* great evil. Therefore in this petition we ask God that He will keep us (*a.*) from all sin and wickedness;" and (*b.*) from our ghostly (spiritual) enemy—our "adversary the devil"—the author of sin; and (*c.*) "from everlasting death," the fruit and punishment of sin (Rom. vi. 21, 23; St. James i. 15).

See 2 Tim. iv. 18; 2 Thess. iii. 3; St. John xvii. 15.

Amen (verily).—"And this I trust He will do of His mercy and goodness, through our Lord Jesus Christ" (in whose name, since His Ascension into heaven as our Mediator and Advocate, all acceptable prayer must be offered), (St. John xiv. 12, 13, xvi. 23; 1 Tim. ii. 5; Heb. iv. 15, 16); and according to whose will and teaching we thus pray. He told us so to ask (1 St. John v. 14, 15); "and therefore I say, Amen"—that is, "So be it" (or, "So may it be"), (1 Cor. xiv. 16; Ps. lxxii. 19, cvi. 48).

In St. Matthew's Gospel there is added before Amen the Doxology or Ascription of Praise, "For thine is the kingdom and the power and the glory for ever" (1 Chron. xxix. 11; 1 Tim. i. 17; St. Jude 25; Rev. vii. 12, xix. 1). In these words we are invited, for our encouragement, to remember that inasmuch as our Father in heaven rules over all, He has power to grant all that we ask (Eph. iii. 20, 21; Rom. xvi. 25; St. Jude 24); and also that all the glory and praise for what we have and are are due to Him alone (Ps. cxv. 1; 1 St. Peter iv. 11; 1 Cor. x. 31).

---

* The Revised Version renders "from the evil one," probably correctly. "Evil," however, as the word is expounded in the Catechism, includes the evil one.

PART V.

THE SACRAMENTS.

HOW WE MAY LOOK TO RECEIVE GRACE TO ENABLE US FOR OUR DUTIES.

THE ordinances or channels through which God is generally pleased to send us grace or spiritual help, in answer to our prayers, are called "the means of grace" (General Thanksgiving). Just as when we want water, we go to the tap at the end of the pipe which brings it from the cistern, or let down a bucket into a well to draw the water up out of it, so do we have recourse to the means which God has appointed, and expect through them to receive the supply of our spiritual need. We read our Bibles, and go to Church, and hear Sermons, and use Sacraments. And we must not expect to get the help we ask if we neglect these; we must, however, always remember that the grace is not *in* them, though it comes *through* them. We must seek it from God by faith while we use them. His Holy Spirit alone can make them bring blessings to us.

If I ask God for health and strength of body, and neglect to take my meals, and keep myself clean, and breathe fresh air, and wear suitable clothing, I cannot expect to keep well and strong, however earnestly I pray. And yet I may do all these things, and without God's blessing they may not avail to maintain my health.

Such "means of grace" are prayer in its influence upon ourselves, apart from what it obtains for us: the reading of the Bible, public worship, preaching and teaching, meditation, self-examination, and active work for Christ and for others.

There are, however, two "means of grace" which have a distinctive character and special importance, as directly instituted by Christ, which are called Sacraments. Of these the Catechism goes on to speak.

Let us suppose that you have prayed to God to make you strong to resist temptation, or bear trial, or correct a fault. You read your Bible or hear a sermon, and you learn something more of God's love to you, or you go to the Lord's Table, and have Christ's love in dying for you brought home to you more strongly, and you go away feeling more love to Him who so loved you, and thus more strong to resist temptation, or bear trial patiently for His sake, or to correct the fault which is displeasing to Him. You *have received* the help or grace you needed, and called for by prayer.

Q. "How many Sacraments hath Christ ordained (or appointed) in His Church?"

Ans. "Two only, as generally necessary to salvation—that is to say, Baptism, and the Supper of the Lord."

These are necessary to salvation *generally*, that is—in the old sense of the word for men in *general*—for all, if they would continue in a state of safety, "where they may be had."* We dare not limit God to the use of any means, as if He were tied to them and could not save without them, though He is pleased commonly to employ them; but *we* are tied to them, and must not look for salvation if we wilfully neglect their use.† Wilful neglect is sacrilegious presumption.

"Two only." See Article XXV., 3rd paragraph, and "Homily of Common Prayer and Sacraments."

There were two similar divinely appointed ordinances in the Jewish Church—Circumcision, by which the Israelites were admitted into covenant with God (Gen. xvii. 7, 9-12), and the Passover whereby they commemorated their deliverance (or redemption) from bondage in Egypt (Exod. xii. 25-28, xiii. 8). In Col. ii. 11, 12 (R.V.), St. Paul seems to call Baptism "the circumcision of Christ." In 1 Cor. v. 7, 8 (R.V.), he says: "Our Passover also hath been sacrificed, even Christ, wherefore let us keep (be keeping) the feast."

Q. "What meanest thou by this word *Sacrament?*" ‡

---

* "Beloved, ye hear in this Gospel (St. John iii. 1-9) the express words of our Saviour Christ, that except a man be born of water and of the Spirit, he cannot enter into the kingdom of God. Whereby ye may perceive *the great necessity* of this Sacrament, *where it may be had.* Likewise," &c.—Exhortation in Office of Adult Baptism.

† "All Christians have a right to them: nor may any, without hazard of missing of these graces (which they are ordained to convey and to assure us of), refuse to use them, who have the opportunity of being partakers of them" (see St. John iii. 5; St. Mark xvi. 16; 1 Cor. xi. 24).—Archbishop Wake.

‡ Sacrament, from a Latin word, which might mean any sacred thing, but came to be used for a sacred oath, like the oath of allegiance taken by a Roman soldier.

Ans. "I mean an outward and visible sign of an inward and spiritual grace given unto us, ordained by Christ Himself, as a means whereby we receive the same, and a pledge to assure us thereof."

A Sacrament, then, must have—

1. An outward sign to represent visibly something which we cannot see. Such signs are water and bread and wine.

This is also called "the outward element" (Nowell's Catechism), or "the matter" (Ministration of Private Baptism).

2. An inward and spiritual grace, or gift of God *to the soul* (which is *represented* by the sign), through the inward operation *of the* Holy Spirit. Such are Regeneration and the Body and Blood of Christ.

("Outward" and "inward" do not here mean relative to one another, but *to us*.)

3. Christ's own appointment or institution, "ordained by Christ Himself." Christ ordained Baptism immediately before His Ascension. (See St. Matt. xxviii. 18, 19; St. Mark xvi. 15, 16.) He instituted the Lord's Supper in the upper chamber before His death. (See 1 Cor. xi 23-26.)

This sign must also be—

4. A means (way or channel) whereby (by which) we receive the same (grace)—the thing-signified by the sign. Sacraments are "means of grace," conveying to those who receive them, rightly or worthily, the grace which they represent. They are "*effectual signs*," by which God "doth work invisibly in us," and doth not only quicken (stimulate, "*excitat*," Latin), but also strengthen and confirm our faith in Him (Art. XXV.).

5. It must also be a pledge to assure us thereof (of this)—of the bestowal of the grace signified. A pledge is something given as a security that a promise or engagement will be kept. Sacraments are "certain sure witnesses ... of grace and God's good-will towards us" (Art. XXV.). "He hath instituted and ordained holy mysteries as *pledges* of His love" (Exhortation in "The Communion").

The brazen serpent (Num. xxi. 8, 9) was a *means* of healing to the Israelites. Washing in the River Jordan was a means of cleansing to Naaman (2 Kings v. 10, 14). It was God who healed them, and He could have done this without the use of these means, but He was pleased to appoint them as the way of obtaining a cure, and therefore they became necessary.

The rainbow was given to Noah as a *pledge* or token of God's covenant that the world should not again be destroyed by the waters of a flood (Gen. ix. 12-18). See also instances of a pledge given in Gideon's fleece (Judges vi. 36-40), and the return of the shadow on the sun-dial of Ahaz (2 Kings xx. 8-11).

In the Marriage Service, the Ring is said to be "a token and pledge" of the vow and covenant made between "the man and the woman."

The anointing with oil of persons chosen and called to the offices of prophet, priest, or king among the Jews was an outward and visible *sign* of the gift of the Holy Spirit to qualify those who were called for their office. It was also a *pledge* to assure them of that gift, and also a *means* by which that gift was bestowed. See in the case of David (1 Sam. xvi. 1, 13), "The Spirit of the Lord came upon David from that day forward."

The definition of a Sacrament may be thus paraphrased. Something material and visible, which, in its appointed use, is a sign of, or represents to us, a spiritual and invisible grace, or gift of God to the soul, which sign has been given to us* by the appointment of Christ Himself; a means (medium or channel) by which we may receive the grace represented, and also a pledge to assure all who receive it rightly ("the faithful") of its bestowal.

* It is the sign which is given unto us. The comma should be after "grace" and before "given." So it is found in the MS. annexed to the Act of Uniformity, and in the sealed copies of the Prayer-Book. The earliest Welsh Prayer-Book (1664), and the earliest Latin translation (1670), also show that "given" belongs, equally with "ordained," to "sign," not "grace." The altered punctuation of the Catechism, as generally printed in the present day, is entirely unauthorised. The words "given unto us" thus exclude from the definition of a "Sacrament" the "reserved host," the unused (though consecrated) water in the font, and the wine which is withheld from lay communicants.

They also exclude "sacrifice," *i.e.*, something given by man *to* God, from the definition of "this word Sacrament." A Sacrament is something given *by* God *to* man. (Compare Rom. iv. 11; Acts vii. 8; Ezek. xx. 12; Isa. vii. 14.)

(See "Notes on the Book of Common Prayer," by Dr. A. J. Stephens, vol. iii. p. 1463; and the same author's "Irish Prayer-Book of 1665," p. 512 (Ecclesiastical History Society); and also a full discussion of the whole question in a pamphlet entitled "The Misprinted Catechism," by J. T. Tomlinson. J. F. Shaw & Co.)

"Sacraments ordained of Christ be not only badges or tokens of Christian men's profession, but rather they be certain sure witnesses and effectual signs of grace and God's good-will towards us, by the which He doth work invisibly in us, and doth not only quicken, but also strengthen and confirm, our faith in Him" (Art. XXV.).

"A Sacrament . . . is a visible sign of an invisible grace, that is to say, that setteth out to the eyes and other outward senses the inward working of God's free mercy, and doth, as it were, seal in our hearts the promises of God."—Homily of Common Prayer and Sacraments.

"*M.* What meanest thou by this word Sacrament?"

"*S.* I meane an outward and visible signe representing an inward and inuisible spirituall grace, ordeined by Christ him selfe, to testifie God's good will and bountifulnesse towardes us through the same Christ our Sauiour; by the which, God's promises touching forgeuenes of sinnes and eternal saluation geuen through Christ, are, as it were, sealed, and the truth of them is more certainly confirmed in our hartes."—Nowell's Little Catechism, p. 19 (Dublin, M'Gee).

Q. "How many parts are there in a Sacrament?"

Ans. "Two: the outward visible sign, and the inward spiritual grace."

The definition of the *word* Sacrament is a sign of grace. "Sacrament" seems to be here used in a loose sense for the rite or ordinance.

These are always to be distinguished, and not confused. "Transubstantiation (or the change of the substance of bread and wine) in the Supper of the Lord . . . overthroweth the nature of a Sacrament" (Art. XXVIII.).

"The Sacraments (1) represent; (2) exhibit; (3) seal.

"1. They represent and set before our eyes, under corporal and visible elements, what Christ hath done for us. For example, the bread broken —Christ's Body crucified; and the wine poured out—His Blood shed for us. And in this respect they are called signs and monuments of His love—signs of heavenly things.

"2. But this is not all, for they exhibit also. In them that grace is truly given which by the signs is represented. All indeed receive not the grace of God that receive the Sacraments of grace. But by them grace is offered to all the Church, though exhibi ed only to the faithful; for upon the performance of this order He actually makes over and conveys so much grace and favour unto us as at that time is useful for us.

"3. They are pledges to assure us of this grace. For the Sacrament is as it were a power left us by God in the hand of the minister, to give us acquiescence and ground of confidence that the graces promised shall be surely performed. Of which that we doubt the less, it is called a seal.

For God, not content with the general offer of His promises, out of His mere mercy, hath thought fit to seal them to every particular believer, having a regard thereby to their infirmity."—Bishop Nicholson's *Exposition of the Catechism*, pp. 155, 156. Oxford, Parker.

I. The Sacrament of Baptism.

(At the beginning of the Catechism Baptism is regarded as "a sign of profession, and mark of difference" (Art. XXVII.); as the appointed mode of entrance into the Christian Covenant, and of admission into the Church. Here it is treated of as a means of grace.)

Q. "What is the outward visible sign or form in Baptism?"

Ans. "Water, wherein the person is baptized *in the Name of the Father, and of the Son, and of the Holy Ghost.*"

To baptize originally means to wash, and Baptism means washing with water. When a person is baptized, he is dipped under water or water is poured over him.

This is done "in," or rather "into" (R.V., St. Matt. xxviii. 19), the Name (not names—indicating the unity of the Three Persons, of the Father, and of the Son, and of the Holy Ghost). Our Lord's words express the new relationship to the Three Divine Persons into which we are formally admitted in Baptism, and the belief in and reliance upon Them for salvation to which we are pledged (Eph. ii. 18). "The first act of admission into the Church thus involves recognition of the fundamental principle of all dogmatic truth."—*Speaker's Commentary*, on St. Matt. xxviii. 19.*

Q. "What is the inward and spiritual grace?"

Ans. "A death unto sin, and a new birth unto righteousness: for being by nature born in sin and the children of wrath, we are hereby made the children of grace."

* The Church of England holds that the only two requisites for the valid administration of this Sacrament are the use of water and of this form of words. (See questions in Private Baptism of Children.) As to the mode of using the water, we have no directions in the Bible. In warm climates, and in the early ages of the Church, immersion or dipping was doubtless the prevalent practice. In colder climates pouring water or sprinkling has always been held sufficient. Our Church, regarding the question as of little consequence, directs, "If the godfathers and godmothers shall certify the priest that the child may well endure it, he shall dip it in the water discreetly and warily, but if they certify that the child is weak, it shall suffice to pour water upon it" (Rubric in Public Baptism of Infants). In the case of an adult, it is merely directed, "The Priest . . . then shall dip him in the water, or pour water upon him."

The application of water represents the washing away of sin. As water makes the body clean, and "puts away the filth of the flesh" (1 St. Peter iii. 21), so is the soul washed from sin by the Blood of Jesus and the "renewing of the Holy Ghost" (Titus iii. 5). Hence the forgiveness of sin is frequently spoken of as "washing" (Ps. li. 2, 7; Ezek. xxxvi. 25; 1 Cor. vi. 11). Ceasing from, or forsaking, sin is also spoken of as washing oneself (Isa. i. 16; Jer. iv. 14; Ps. xxvi. 6).

Baptism is therefore described as a washing away of sin (Acts xxii. 16), as "the washing of regeneration" (Titus iii. 5), because in it water has been "sanctified to the mystical (symbolical) washing away of sin." It thus represents "a death unto sin and a new birth unto righteousness." Baptism by immersion, or dipping under the water, is a lively figure of this. When the person thus baptized is buried under the water and disappears out of sight, his death and burial with Christ to sin is represented; and when he comes up again out of the water, his rising again with Christ to a new life is represented (Rom. vi. 4, 5).

"The secret and spiritual grace is of two sorts—that is, forgiveness of sins and regeneration; both of which in the same outward sign have their full and express resemblance.

"First, as the uncleannesses of the body are washed away with water, so the spots of the soul are washed away by forgiveness of sins. Secondly, the beginning of regeneration—that is, the mortifying of our nature, is expressed by dipping in the water or by sprinkling of it. Finally, when we by and by rise up again out of the water, under which we be for a short time, the new life, which is the other part and the end of our regeneration, is thereby represented."—Nowell's Larger Catechism (Parker Society), pp. 207, 208.*

---

* What follows is well worthy to be here quoted.

"*M.* Thou seemest to make the water but a certain figure of divine things.

"*S.* It is a figure indeed, but not empty or deceitful, but such as hath the truth of the things themselves joined and knit unto it. For as in Baptism God truly delivereth us forgiveness of sins and newness of life, so do we certainly receive them. For God forbid that we should think that God mocketh and deceiveth us with vain figures.

"*M.* Do we then obtain forgiveness of sins by the outward washing or sprinkling of water?

"*S.* No. For only Christ hath with His blood washed, and clean washed, away the spots of our souls. This honour, therefore, it is not

The following are the words of Holy Scripture as to the grace of Baptism :—" Be baptized . . . in the name of Jesus Christ *for the remission of sins*, and ye shall receive the gift of the Holy Ghost " (Acts ii. 38). " Be baptized and wash away thy sins, calling on the name of the Lord " (Acts xxii. 16).

" We, who died to sin, how shall we live any longer therein? Or are ye ignorant that all we who were baptized into Christ were baptized into His death? We were buried therefore with Him through baptism into death ; that like as Christ was raised from the dead through the glory of the Father, so we also might walk in newness of life " (Rom. vi. 2-5, R.V.).

See also vers. 5-15.

" Having been buried with Him in Baptism, wherein we were also raised with Him through faith in the working of God, who raised Him from the dead " (Col. ii. 12, R.V.).

In the Exhortation to the Godparents at the close of "The Public Baptism of Infants," we are taught to remember always " that Baptism doth represent unto us our profession (as Christians) ; which is, to follow the example of our Saviour Christ, and to be made like unto Him ; that as He died and rose again for us, so should we, who are baptized, die from sin, and rise again unto righteousness, continually mortifying all our evil and corrupt affections, and daily proceeding in all virtue and godliness of living."

" Baptism is not only a sign of profession and mark of difference, whereby Christian men are discerned from others that be not christened, but it is also a sign of regeneration or new birth, whereby, as by an instrument, they that receive Baptism rightly are grafted into the Church ; the promises of forgiveness of sin, and of our adoption to be the sons of

---

lawful to give to the outward element. But the Holy Ghost, as it were, sprinkling our consciences with that holy blood, wiping away all the spots of sins, maketh us clean before God. Of this cleansing of our sins we have a seal and pledge in the Sacrament.

" *M.* But whence have we regeneration?

" *S.* None other ways but from the death and resurrection of Christ. For by the force of Christ's death our old man is, after a certain manner, crucified and mortified, and the corruptness of our nature is, as it were, buried, that it no more live and be strong in us. And by the beneficial means of His resurrection He giveth us grace to be newly formed unto a new life, to obey the righteousness of God.

" *M.* Do all generally, and without difference, receive this grace?

" *S.* The only faithful receive this fruit : but the unbelieving, in refusing the promises offered them by God, shut up the entry against themselves, and go away empty. Yet do they not thereby make that the Sacraments lose their force and nature."—Nowell's Larger Catechism (Parker Society), p. 208.

God by the Holy Ghost, are visibly signed and sealed: Faith is confirmed and Grace increased by virtue of prayer unto God. The Baptism of young children is in any wise to be retained in the Church, as most agreeable with the institution of Christ" (Art. XXVII.).

"The effect of Baptism is yet more plainly shown"* in the explanation which follows. It teaches that we are "by nature born in sin" (with a sinful and corrupt nature inherited from our parents)—

"Behold I was shapen in iniquity, and in sin did my mother conceive me" (Ps. li. 5).
"Who can bring a clean thing out of an unclean? Not one" (Job xiv. 4).
"Through one man sin entered into the world, and death through sin, and so death passed unto all men, for that all sinned." "Through the one man's disobedience the many were made sinners" (Rom. v. 12, 19, R.V.).

"And the children of wrath" (that is, deserving only of and liable to God's anger or holy hatred of sin)—

"We all ... were by nature children of wrath, even as the rest" (Eph. ii. 3, R.V.; Rom. i. 18, viii. 7, 8; Eph. v. 6; Col. iii. 6).
"Original sin ... is the fault and corruption of the nature of every man, that naturally is engendered of the offspring of Adam; whereby man is very far gone from original righteousness, and is of his own nature inclined to evil, so that the flesh lusteth always contrary to the spirit, and therefore in every person born into this world it deserveth God's wrath and damnation" (Art. IX.).

"(But) we are hereby" (by the new birth unto righteousness, of which Baptism is the sign and pledge) "made the children of grace" (admitted into God's favour, into a state of salvation, in which we are made members of Christ, the children of God, and inheritors of the kingdom of heaven, through the undeserved grace or gift of God alone).

"Not by works of righteousness which we have done, but according to His mercy He saved us, by the washing of regeneration and renewing of the Holy Ghost; which He shed on us abundantly, through Jesus Christ

---

* Nowell's Catechism.

our Saviour; that, being justified by His grace, we should be made heirs according to the hope of eternal life" (Titus iii. 5-8).

See also Eph. ii. 1-10.

"Where by nature we are the children of wrath, and none of God's Church or household, we are by Baptism received into the Church, and assured that we are now the children of God, and joined and grafted into the body of Christ, and become His members, and do grow into one body with Him."—Nowell's Second Catechism.

2. What is required of persons to be baptized?

What must they have in order that Baptism may be really a means of grace to them? for in such *only* as *worthily receive* the same (Sacraments), they have a wholesome effect or operation (Art. XXV.).

Ans. (1.) Repentance, whereby they forsake sin. This is the same as renunciation of the devil, the world, and the flesh. (See Part I. p. 10.)

(Then Peter said unto them), "Repent and be baptized every one of you in the name of Jesus Christ for the remission of sins" (Acts ii. 38).

(Jesus) said unto them, "Thus it is written (and that it behoved) Christ to suffer and to rise from the dead the third day: and that repentance and remission of sins should be preached in His name among all nations beginning at Jerusalem" (St. Luke xxiv. 46, 47). (This is apparently St. Luke's account of the Apostolic commission, which in St. Matt. xxviii. 19, and St. Mark xvi. 15, 16, mentions Baptism.)

Repentance is a change of heart and mind as to sin. It is not merely sorrow for sin, but it is the fruit of "godly sorrow," or sorrow towards God—sorrow for having offended God (2 Cor. vii. 9, 10; Ps. li. 3, 4). It leads not only to turn from sin, but also to turn to God for forgiveness and help, "intending to lead a new life, following the commandments of God, and walking from henceforth in His holy ways."

"Let the wicked *forsake* His way, and the unrighteous man His thoughts: and let him return unto the Lord, and He will have mercy upon him; and to our God, for He will abundantly pardon" (Isa. lv. 7).

"Wash you, make you clean; *put away* the evil of your doings from before mine eyes; *cease* to do evil; learn to do well" (Isa. i. 16, 17; see v. 18).

"I send thee (to the Gentiles) . . . to turn them *from* darkness *to* light, and *from* the power of Satan *unto* God, that they may receive forgiveness of sins, and inheritance among them which are sanctified by faith that is in me" (Acts xxvi. 18).

(2.) And Faith, whereby they stedfastly (firmly and perseveringly) believe the promises of God made to them in that Sacrament." These are "the promises of forgiveness of sin, and of our adoption to be the sons of God by the Holy Ghost," which "are visibly signed and sealed" by Baptism (Art. XXVII.).

"Be baptized every one of you in the name of Jesus Christ unto the remission of your sins, and ye shall receive the gift of the Holy Ghost. For to you is the promise, and to your children, and to all that are afar off, even as many as the Lord our God shall call unto Him. . . . They then that received His word were baptized" (Acts ii. 38-42, R.V.).

(That this means the same as to "believe all the Articles of the Christian Faith," is shown in Part I. p. 17.)

"Jesus came preaching the Gospel of the kingdom of God, and saying, The time is fulfilled, and the kingdom of God is at hand: repent ye and believe the Gospel" (St. Mark i. 14, 15).
"If thou shalt confess with thy mouth the Lord Jesus, and shalt believe in thine heart that God hath raised Him from the dead, thou shalt be saved. For with the heart man believeth unto righteousness; and with the mouth confession is made unto salvation" (Rom. x. 9, 10).
"Testifying both to Jews and Greeks repentance toward God and faith toward our Lord Jesus Christ" (Acts xx. 21).
"Sirs, what must I do to be saved? And they said, Believe on the Lord Jesus, and thou shalt be saved, thou and thy house. And they spake the word of the Lord unto him, and all that were in his house. And he took them the same hour of the night, and washed their stripes, and was baptized, he and all his, immediately" (Acts xvi. 30-33).

The reason why obedience is not mentioned as required is because it is the after result or fruit of faith, which is manifested by and always leads to obedience. See this illustrated by the example of Abraham (St. James ii. 14-25). "Good works are the fruits of faith, and follow after justification" (Art. XII.).

Infant Baptism.—If repentance and faith are required,
Q. Why, then, are infants baptized, when by reason of their tender (young and helpless, Gen. xxxiii. 13) age they cannot perform them? (*i.e.*, repentance and faith).

Ans. Because they (infants) promise them both (both of these, *i.e.*, repentance and faith) by their sureties (godparents), which promise (of repentance and faith made in their name), when they come to age ("the years of discretion"—Preface to Order of

Confirmation) themselves (the baptized infants), are bound to perform.*

"*They* promise." It is the infants who make the promise *by* their sureties, who speak in their name. ("Wilt *thou* be baptized ?" "That is *my* desire ").† The godparents do not undertake to do these things for the child. Their parts and duties are to see that he is taught to know, so soon as he shall be able to learn, what he has promised by them ; and that he be brought up to lead a godly and a Christian life.

Children are therefore called upon by the Church, when they have come to years, and have learned what their godfathers and godmothers promised for them in Baptism, "themselves with their own mouth and consent, openly before the Church to ratify and confirm the same ; and also to promise that by the grace of God they will evermore endeavour themselves faithfully to observe such things as they, by their own confession, have assented unto" (Preface to Order of Confirmation).

They do this in Confirmation, which is the fitting complement of Infant Baptism, and the prescribed mode of admission to the privilege of participation in the other Sacrament—the Lord's Supper.

The answer in Nowell's Larger Catechism (Parker Society, p. 209) is : "That faith and repentance go before Baptism, is required only in persons so grown in years that by age they are capable of both. But to infants the promise made to the Church by Christ, in whose faith they are baptized, shall for the present time be sufficient; and then afterwards, when they are grown to years, they must needs themselves acknowledge the truth of their baptism, and have the force thereof to be lively in their souls, and to be represented in their life and behaviours." ‡

(The questions and answers which follow, and give the reasons for Infant Baptism, are well worth attention.)

---

* The practice of infant baptism was anterior to the institution of sponsorship, and there is no provision for sponsors in private baptism. Neither the validity nor grace of baptism depends upon this promise made by the sureties.

† We have instances of such vicarious promises and undertakings (Josh. xxiv. 15 ; 1 Sam. i. 28).

‡ This suggests how (Infant) Baptism may be a continual means of grace in adult years. The following directions from Nicholson on the Catechism (Oxford, Parker), p. 165, are very valuable :—

"Baptism is of special use through a Christian's whole life. It is but

"The Baptism of young children is in any wise to be retained in the Church as most agreeable with the institution of Christ" (Art. XXVII.). We believe this, because: (1.) Children, when eight days old, were circumcised, and thus admitted into covenant with God (and "seeing that it is certain that the grace of God is both more plentifully poured and more clearly declared in the Gospel by Christ, than at that time it was in the Old Testament by Moses, it were a great indignity if the same grace should now be thought to be either obscurer or in any part abated" (Nowell as above). (2.) Our Lord took and blessed little children, and said, "Of such is the kingdom of God" (St. Mark x. 13-17). (3.) He commanded the Apostles to baptize all nations, making no exceptions; and we read that they baptized whole households in which there must have been infants and young children (Acts xvi. 15, 33; 1 Cor. i. 16). (4.) St. Paul declares that the children of Christian parents are "holy," and may therefore be fitly dedicated to God in Baptism (1 Cor. vii. 14). (5.) The Baptism of infants has been the practice in the Christian Church from the earliest ages (1 Cor. xi. 16).

II. The Sacrament of the Lord's Supper.

1. **The Design of its Institution.**—For account of its institution see St. Matt. xxvi. 26, &c.; St. Mark xiv. 22, &c.; St. Luke xxii. 19, &c.; and especially 1 Cor. xi. 23-27 (which read carefully).

Q. "Why was the Sacrament of the Lord's Supper ordained?"

Ans. "For the continual remembrance of the sacrifice of the death of Christ, and of the benefits which we receive thereby (by that death)."

(*a.*) It was designed to be "continual"—of perpetual obliga-

once administered; but the virtue and efficacy thereof grows not old by time.

"(1.) In all thy fears and doubts, look to thy Baptism and the promises of God then sealed to thee. Lay hold on them by faith, and thou mayest have actual comfort.

"(2.) In thy failings, slips, and revolts, to recover the sooner, look back to thy Baptism. New Baptism shall not need; the covenant and seal of God stands firm, and changeth not.

"(3.) Renew thy repentance; renew thy faith in those blessed promises of grace, sealed and secured in Baptism, and then expect all good from God's free mercies in Christ, although thy performances fall very short, though thou act an unprofitable servant." See also quotations from Ussher ("Body of Divinity," chap. xlii. ed. 1541) in Moule's "Outlines of Christian Doctrine," p. 246, and that writer's own words, p. 254.

tion * and constant use.† This is shown by St. Paul's words, "I have received of the Lord (as a direct revelation) that which also *I delivered unto* you," &c. (1 Cor. xi. 23); and "Ye do show the Lord's death *till He come*" (ver. 26); and by the directions which he gives to the Corinthians as to the manner in which *they* were to eat of that bread and drink of that cup (ver. 27, &c.); also by the practice of the early Church. (See Acts ii. 42, xx. 7, &c.)

(*b*.) For the remembrance of (the sacrifice of the death of) Christ, "This do in remembrance of me" (St. Luke xxii. 19; 1 Cor. xi. 24). "This do ye as oft as ye drink it, in remembrance of Me" (1 Cor. xi. 25); and especially of His death, "As often as ye eat this bread and drink this cup, ye proclaim the Lord's death" (1 Cor. xi. 26, R.V.), (the Greek word translated "show" or proclaim, καταγγέλλειν, frequently used in the New Testament, invariably means to tell news to human hearers, "Ye proclaim or preach to each other and to the world"). The words of our Lord plainly refer to His death, "This is my Body, which is *given for* you;" literally "being given." "This cup is the new Covenant in my Blood, even that which is *poured out for* you;" literally "being poured out" (St. Luke xxii. 19, 20, R.V.), or "which is *shed* for many" (St. Matt. xxvi. 28; St. Mark xiv. 24).

Hence we may learn the unspeakable importance of the *death* of the Lord Jesus, seeing that it is His *death* which He would have us especially remember: for that death is not only the proof of His love toward us— "His exceeding great love in thus dying for us" (St. John xv. 13; Rom. v. 8; Gal. ii. 20; 1 St. John iv. 9, 10)—but also the means by which our eternal life was procured (St. John vi. 35). This is what is meant when Christ's death is said to be a *sacrifice*.

"The sacrifice of the death of Christ." His Body was given *for* us, and the Blood shed *for* us. The death of Christ was not only the death of a good man, or of a martyr (who dies to attest the truth of his teaching), but the death of One who bare our sins in His own body on the tree (1 St. Peter ii. 24); who gave

---

* "He did institute, and in His Holy Gospel *command us to continue* a perpetual memory of that His precious death."—Prayer of Consecration.

† "That as in Baptism we are born again, so with the Lord's Supper we may alway be fed and sustained to spiritual and everlasting life: and therefore it is enough to be once baptized; but as we need oft to be fed, so is the Lord's Supper oft to be received."—Nowell's Second Catechism. See also Hooker's "Ecclesiastical Polity," Book V. chap. lvii. 6; lxvii. 1.

His life a ransom for many (St. Matt. xx. 28). See Isa. liii. 6-13; Heb. ix. 26-28, x. 12-14; 1 St. John ii. 2; 1 Cor. v. 7.

His Blood was "shed for many unto remission of sins" (St. Matt. xxvi. 28, R.V.). He suffered "death upon the cross for our redemption, who made there (by His one oblation of Himself once offered) a full, perfect, and sufficient sacrifice, oblation, and satisfaction for the sins of the whole world" (Prayer of Consecration in "The Communion").* See pp. 35, 36.

"And (for the remembrance) of the benefits which we receive thereby"—"the innumerable benefits which by His precious blood-shedding He hath obtained to us" (Exhortation in Communion Service). These are summed up in the words, "We obtain remission of sins, and are made partakers of the kingdom of heaven" (Exhortation giving Warning); or in the one word Redemption, "The Supper of the Lord is . . . a Sacrament of our redemption by Christ's death" (Art. XXVIII.).

The blessings which come to us through the blood, or death, of Christ are declared to be Forgiveness (Eph. i. 7); Justification (Rom. v. 9); Reconciliation (Eph. ii. 13); Adoption (Gal. iv. 4, 5); Holiness (Heb. x. 10; Gal. vi. 14); Cleansing of conscience (Heb. ix. 14); Eternal inheritance (Heb. ix. 15).

The design of the Lord's Supper, "that we should alway *remember,*" &c., is constantly kept before us in our Communion Service, *e.g.*, "to be by them received in *remembrance of* His meritorious Cross and Passion" (First Exhortation giving Warning).

"It is your duty to receive the Communion *in remembrance* of the sacrifice of His death, as He Himself hath commanded" (Second Exhortation giving Warning). "To the end that we should alway *remember* the exceeding great love of our Master and only Saviour Jesus Christ, thus dying for us, and the immediate benefits which by His precious blood-shedding He hath obtained to us; He hath instituted and ordained holy mysteries as pledges of His love, and for a continual *remembrance* of His death, to our great and endless comfort" (Exhortation at the Time of the Celebration).

He "did institute and in His Holy Gospel command us to continue a perpetual *memory* of that His precious death." "Grant that we receiving these Thy creatures of bread and wine . . . in *remembrance* of His death and Passion" (Prayer of Consecration).

"Take and eat this *in remembrance* that Christ died for thee."

---

* See "The Doctrine of the Death of Christ," by Rev. N. Dimock. Elliot Stock.

"Drink this *in remembrance* that Christ's Blood was shed for thee" (Words of Administration).*

---

* In none of these passages, nor elsewhere in the Order of the Administration, can the idea of a memorial offered to, or presented before, God be discovered ; nor can it, I believe, be found in Scripture, although the use in the Old Testament of the words translated "do" and "remembrance" is considered by many to countenance this view. As to the former, however ($\pi o\iota \epsilon \hat{\iota} \nu$), which, it is said, may be rendered "offer" (this), it is never used elsewhere in the New Testament with a sacrificial meaning ; and the proposed rendering is of only recent origin. (See note in Mason's "Faith of the Gospel," p. 328, crown 8vo edition.) The sense in which the other word ($\dot{a}\nu\acute{a}\mu\nu\eta\sigma\iota s$) is used is determined by the term employed by the Apostle to describe what they do who eat this bread and drink this cup ; they "proclaim" (R.V.) or preach Christ's death, words which it is to be noted are connected with the former verse ending "in remembrance of me," by the conjunction "for," intimating that what follows explains the remembrance (1 Cor. xi. 25, 26). The verb $\dot{a}\nu a\mu\iota\mu\nu\acute{\eta}\sigma\kappa\epsilon\iota\nu$, in every case in which it is used in the New Testament (as in classical authors), has manifest reference to something which is to be kept in memory by men, and not pleaded before God. At best this would be very slender foundation on which to base a theory which has no other support in Scripture ; and which, as shown above, finds no countenance from our Church (see also the Articles and Homilies). It is said that as our Lord continually pleads this sacrifice in heaven for us, so we (or the priest for us) in celebrating the Holy Eucharist, join in that pleading, and present before God a memorial of the death of Christ. The teaching, however, of the Epistle to the Hebrews to the effect that Christ, having once offered, for ever sat down (x. 12), ("He sitteth at the right hand of God"), forbids us to entertain the idea of any repetition of the "one oblation once offered." This finds no countenance from, but is rather in direct contradiction to, the teaching of Scripture. "It is true," remarks Bishop Thirlwall in his "Charge," 1869, vol. ii. p. 246, "that the Greek verb in the Septuagint often has the sense of *sacrifice* or *offer ;* but only when the noun which it governs signifies that which is a *victim* or *offering*, and thus determines the sense of the verb. But in the words of institution that which we render "this," has no such sense except on the hypothesis which is to be demonstrated. Equally arbitrary is the sense attached to the word *remembrance* as implying sacrifice, which must always depend on the context. The view which our Church takes of this point seems sufficiently evident from the words which she uses in the delivery of the consecrated elements. She nowhere indicates any other. He further remarks : "It is not to any transaction which is taking place in the heavenly sanctuary that the Church turns our thoughts in the Prayer of Consecration, but to that which took place in the guest-chamber at Jerusalem at the institution of the Lord's Supper." (p. 245).

Q. "What is the outward part or sign of the Lord's Supper?"
Ans. "Bread and wine, which the Lord hath commanded to be received."

Bread and wine—the ordinary food of the Jews (Ps. civ. 14, 15; Gen. xiv. 18; Judges xix. 19; Neh. v. 15; St. Luke vii. 33), and employed in the feast of the Passover—are types of the necessary food of the soul. These "the Lord hath commanded to be *received*" (not offered); we are to "take and eat" (the bread), and to "drink all" (of the cup). "The Sacraments were not ordained of Christ to be gazed upon or to be carried about, but that we should duly use them" (Article XXV.). "The cup of the Lord is not to be denied to the lay people; for both the parts of the Lord's Sacrament, by Christ's ordinance and com-

---

The Lord's Supper, we must remember, was instituted at the Feast of the Passover, of which it was henceforth to take the place. That ordinance was instituted in order to keep in the remembrance of the Israelites God's interposition on their behalf on their deliverance from the house of bondage. With reference to it the direction was given, "Thou shalt *show* thy son in that day, saying, This is *done* because of that which the Lord did unto me when I came forth out of Egypt, and it shall be for a *sign* unto thee upon thine hand, and for a *memorial* between thine eyes" (Exod. xiii. 8, 9). This reply to the son as to the meaning of the feast, which formed a part of its ritual in the days of our Lord, was called "Haggadah," or "showing forth," the very term employed by St. Paul. (See Edersheim's "The Temple, &c., in the Time of Jesus Christ," p. 199, R.T.S.) Note also the use of the words "do" (done) and "memorial," evidently used of something designed to keep the people in remembrance, and not to be presented to the Lord. So in xii. 14: "This day shalt be unto you for a *memorial*." The parallel supplies very helpful illustration, for "Christ our Passover is sacrificed for us; therefore let us keep the feast."

"*M.* Was this supper ordained of Christ to be offered as a sacrifice to God the Father for remission of sins?

"*S.* No; for when Christ died upon the cross, He once fully made that only everlasting sacrifice for our salvation for ever (Heb. vii. 26, &c., ix. 11, &c., x. 9, 10, 12, 14, 18), and hath left nothing for us to do, but thankfully to take the use and benefit of that eternal sacrifice, which we chiefly do in the Lord's Supper" (Nowell's Second Catechism, p. 55).

"We must take heed lest of the memory it be made a sacrifice" (First Part of Homily concerning the Sacrament).

See also a paper by Dr. Plummer in "The Expositor," vol. vii, 3rd Series, p. 441; and "This do in Remembrance of Me," by Professor Abbott of Dublin. Longmans, 1893.

mandment, ought to be *ministered to* all Christian men alike" (Article XXX.).

Q. "What is the inward part or thing signified?"

Ans. "The Body and Blood of Christ, which are verily (truly) and indeed (really) taken and received by the faithful (those who 'draw near with faith') in the Lord's Supper."

"And as they were eating, Jesus took bread, and blessed, and brake it, and He gave to the disciples and said: Take, eat; this is My Body. And He took a cup, and gave thanks, and gave to them, saying, Drink ye all of it; for this is My Blood of the covenant which is shed for many unto remission of sins" (St. Matt. xxvi. 26–29, R.V.).

"The cup of blessing, which we bless, is it not a communion (joint or common participation) of the Blood of Christ? The Bread which we break, is it not a communion of the Body of Christ?" (1 Cor. x. 16, R.V.).

The word "is" plainly means something more than "represents" or "is a sign of," while at the same time it does not imply any change of the substance of bread and wine (Article XXVII.). It rather links the two together as correlated in the way of cause and effect, as in Rom. viii. 10, "The Spirit is life," *i.e.*, "the principle of life," as cause is energy or activity of life as effect. Similarly in these words there is no identity indeed, but there is a certain congruity between God's lesser good or gift of bread, and God's inestimable good or gift of the Body given by Him, and self-given by Christ; for from the earth-born food comes natural nourishment, from the heavenly, spiritual; and there is besides this congruity a correlation also of *cause* and *effect*. So that the meaning seems to be:—This (in effect) is My Body. *How* such instrumental cause produces such effect is to us unknown: but as Hooker says, "That which produceth any certain effect is not improperly *said to be* that very effect whereunto it tendeth, and this usage in language is far from uncommon" (Canon Evans in *Speaker's Commentary*, Note on 1 Cor. xi. 24). Similarly Rev. W. B. Marriott, after an exhaustive examination of the use of the copula in Scripture, explains "is" as meaning "is in power and effect" (*Remains*, p. 225).

Dean Mansel in the *Speaker's Commentary* on St. Matt. xxvi. 26, pertinently remarks, "When these words were uttered, the living Body of the Lord was visibly present before the disciples, distinct from the Bread which He gave to them; and the words must have been understood by them at the time in a sense compatible with this fact."

What is meant by the Body and Blood of Christ? These words represent to us the Incarnation of the Son of God, by which He was made flesh, "partook of flesh and blood" (Heb. ii. 14), and became Man with a truly human body; and His Passion and Death, in which that Body was given for us, and

His Blood shed or poured out for us men and for our salvation. The offer then and gift of the Body (as broken) and Blood (as shed) of Christ is the offer and gift of Himself, and of all that by His Incarnation, His Life, His Death, His Resurrection, and His Ascension He is to us, and has wrought for us.

To "eat" and "drink," to "feed upon," is to take to ourselves, by a voluntary and conscious act, that which is without, so as to assimilate it, and make it part of ourselves. So "to eat the flesh and drink the Blood of the Son of Man" is to "make our own, appropriate, and use the virtue of His humanity as He lived for us, the virtue of His humanity as He died for us" (Westcott, *The Dogmatic Faith*, p. 63). And this we do by faith. Hence eating and drinking are signs and tokens of the way in which we receive these benefits and have our spiritual life sustained.

Our Lord's own words teach us this :—

"I am the Bread of Life: he that *cometh* to Me shall never hunger: and he that *believeth on* Me shall never thirst. If any man *eat* of this Bread, he shall live for ever. Whoso *eateth* My flesh, and *drinketh* My Blood, hath eternal life" (St. John vi. 35, 51, 54). In these passages "coming to" and "believing on" evidently mean the same as "*eating* His flesh," and "drinking His Blood." *

So our Church teaches "the Body of Christ is given, taken, and received in the Supper only after an heavenly and spiritual manner; and the mean whereby the Body of Christ is received and eaten in the Supper *is Faith*" (Article XXVIII.).

Compare the words of Administration, "The Body of our Lord Jesus Christ, which was given for thee, preserve thy body and soul unto everlasting life. Take and eat this (bread) in remembrance that Christ died for thee, and (as you do this) *feed on Him*, in thy *heart*, by faith, with thanksgiving."

See also the plain teaching of the Rubric after the "Communion of the Sick" as to what is necessary in order to eat and drink the Body and Blood of Christ profitably, wherein it is laid down: "If a man (for any just impediment) do not receive the Sacrament of Christ's Body and Blood, the Curate shall instruct him, that if he do truly repent him of his sins, and stedfastly believe that Jesus Christ hath suffered death upon the cross for him, and shed His Blood for his redemption, earnestly remembering the benefits he hath thereby, and giving Him hearty thanks

---

* It is clear that these words cannot be restricted to the Lord's Supper, as they were spoken before it was instituted. It is clear also that they can only apply to those who, in the Lord's Supper, partake by faith.

therefor, he doth eat and drink the Body and Blood of our Saviour Christ profitably to his soul's health, although he do not receive the Sacrament with his mouth."

Whereas in Article XXIX. it is said, "The wicked and such as be void of a lively faith, although they do carnally and visibly press with their teeth the Sacrament of the Body and Blood of Christ, yet in no wise are they partakers of Christ."

"The Body of Christ is given, taken, and eaten in the Supper only after an heavenly and spiritual manner" (Article XXVIII.). When the Jews asked "How can this man give us His flesh to eat?" our Lord replied, "It is the spirit that quickeneth; the flesh profiteth nothing: the words that I have spoken unto you are spirit and are life" (St. John vi. 63, R.V.). The soul, like the body, has its own food, its own appetite for it, and its own way of receiving and digesting it.

Q. "What are the benefits whereof (of which) we are partakers thereby (by the receiving of the Body and Blood of Christ)?"

Ans. "The strengthening and refreshing of our souls by the Body and Blood of Christ, as our bodies are by the Bread and Wine."

The benefits (advantages) which we receive from feeding upon bread and wine are the strengthening ("Bread, which strengtheneth man's heart," Ps. civ. 15) and refreshing ("Wine, that maketh glad the heart of man," *ibid.*) of our bodies. The benefits which we receive from feeding upon the Body and Blood of Christ are the strengthening ("Christ which strengtheneth me," Phil. iv. 13) and refreshing ("I will refresh you," St. Matt. xi. 28, P.B.V.) of our souls. These need to be strengthened to enable them to resist temptation, and persevere in duty; and to be refreshed, under weariness, and distress on account of sin, discouragements, trials, and afflictions.

"By Sacraments God doth work invisibly in us, and doth not only quicken, but also *strengthen* and confirm our faith in Him" (Article XXV.).

"Our souls are strengthened and refreshed naturally by the edifying and consoling thoughts suggested to our minds when we see Jesus Christ evidently set forth crucified amongst us, and supernaturally by the grace of God, to which in this ordinance we obtain a new title, and by which those thoughts are made effectual to our spiritual comfort and improvement" (Archdeacon Sinclair).

It is well to remember that eternal life is *the knowledge of God* (St.

John xvii. 3), and this is not a thing given once for all, but is capable of continual increase: we grow in grace as we grow in the *knowledge of our Lord and Saviour Jesus Christ* (2 St. Peter iii. 18).

Q. "What is required of them who come to the Lord's Supper?" Who are worthy partakers of that Holy Sacrament? To whom is it really a means of grace? for "in such only as worthily receive the same (Sacraments), they have a wholesome effect or operation, but they that receive them unworthily purchase to themselves damnation, as St. Paul saith (Article XXV.)."

Ans. "To examine themselves, whether they repent them truly of their former sins, stedfastly purposing to lead a new life; have a lively faith in God's mercy through Christ, with a thankful remembrance of His death; and be in charity with all men."

Self-examination, at all times a profitable exercise and means of grace, and frequently enjoined in Scripture, *e.g.*—

"Let us search and try our ways, and turn again to the Lord" (Lam. iii. 40).

"Examine yourselves whether ye be in the faith; prove your own selves" (2 Cor. xiii. 5).

"For if our heart condemn us, God is greater than our heart, and knoweth all things. Beloved, if our heart condemn us not, then have we confidence toward God" (1 St. John iii. 20, 21),—

is specially prescribed as the preparation for the Lord's Supper.

"Let a man examine himself, and so let him eat of that bread and drink of that cup" (1 Cor. xi. 28).

This self-examination is to be not merely a formal exercise, but a means of preparation in order to ascertain our fitness ("whether we be true members of Christ"—Nowell's Second Catechism). It serves to call forth a sense of need, and so of value, of Christ and His salvation, and to give us an appetite, as it were, for that heavenly food which is prepared for us. In doing this we "judge (discern, R.V.) ourselves that we be not judged of the Lord" (1 Cor. xi. 31, 32, and Exhortation at the time of Celebration).

"Search and examine your own consciences (and that not lightly, and after the manner of dissemblers with God; but so) that ye may come holy and clean to such a heavenly feast, in the marriage-garment required by God in Holy Scripture, and be received as worthy partakers of that holy Table."—Warning for Celebration. See also the beginning of the Exhortation at the time of the Celebration.

The rule or standard by which we are thus to examine ourselves is God's Word, and especially the Ten Commandments: "Examine your lives and conversations by the rule of God's commandments" (Exhortation giving Warning). It is for this reason that the Decalogue is rehearsed at the beginning of the Holy Communion.

We should employ these as interpreted by our Lord, and explained in "My duty towards God" and "My duty towards my neighbour" (see pp. 38–57).

The character and purpose of this self-examination is further explained (the tokens by which we shall know whether we be true members of Christ), (Nowell's Second Catechism).* It is to ascertain whether we have—

1. **True Repentance.**—"Whether they repent them truly of their former sins." (For the nature of true repentance see p. 76.)

"Whereinsoever ye shall perceive yourselves to have offended, either by will, word, or deed, there to bewail your own sinfulness, and to confess yourselves to Almighty God, with full purpose of amendment of life. 'Repent you of your sins, or else come not to that Holy Table'" (Exhortation giving Warning).

This must be accompanied by steadfast purpose to lead a new life.

"Amend your lives," "Ye that . . . intend to lead a new life, following the commandments of God, and walking from henceforth in His holy ways, draw near" (Communion Service); "Grant that we may ever hereafter serve and please Thee in newness of life" (Confession). "New life" does not necessarily mean a sudden change of life, but the life of "the new man," of one who, risen with Christ, walks in newness of life (Eph. iv. 20-25; 2 Cor. v. 17; Rom. vi. 4).

Unless we know our sins, we shall not feel our need of Christ's death as a sacrifice for sin; unless we are sorry for our sins, we shall not want forgiveness; and unless we hate them, we shall not wish to be saved from them. We must have an appetite for the spiritual food provided for us in the Lord's Supper.

* "It is required of them that would worthily partake of the Lord's Supper, that they examine themselves of their knowledge to discern the Lord's Body, of their faith to feed upon Him, of their repentance, love, and new obedience, lest coming unworthily they eat and drink judgment to themselves" (Shorter Westminster Catechism).

2. **Lively Faith.**—"Have a lively" (that is, living, and therefore fruit-bearing, St. James ii. 14-20) "faith in God's mercy through Christ." "A full trust in God's mercy" (Exhortation giving Warning); a sure persuasion that, for the sake of the meritorious Cross and Passion of His dear Son, He is faithful and just to forgive us our sins, and to cleanse us from all unrighteousness (1 St. John i. 9); and a reliance upon that mercy alone, and not on any goodness or merit of our own, for forgiveness.

Unless I believe that God gave His Son to die for me, that Jesus Christ "loved me, and gave Himself for me" (Gal. ii. 20), the Lord's Supper will convey no strength or comfort to any soul.

"Now it followeth to have with this knowledge a sure and constant faith, not only that the death of Christ is available for the redemption of all the world, for the remission of sins, and reconciliation with God the Father, but also that He hath made upon His cross a full and sufficient sacrifice for *thee*, a perfect cleansing of *thy* sins; so that thou acknowledgest no other Saviour, Redeemer, Mediator, Advocate, Intercessor, but Christ only, and that thou mayest say with the Apostle, that He loved thee and gave Himself for thee. For this is to stick fast to Christ's promise made in His institution, to make Christ thine own, and to applicate (apply) His merits unto thyself" (Homily concerning the Sacrament, Part I.).

Such faith will be attended by "a thankful remembrance of His death," as the means whereby alone that mercy can be extended to us (Col. i. 12-15; Rev. i. 5, v. 12).

"Above all things, ye must give most hearty thanks to God the Father, the Son, and the Holy Ghost, for the redemption of the world by the death and Passion of our Saviour Christ, both God and Man; who did humble Himself, even to the death upon the Cross, for us miserable sinners, who lay in darkness and the shadow of death that He might make us the children of God, and exalt us to everlasting life" (Exhortation at the time of Holy Communion).

True thankfulness will be shown by our "submitting ourselves wholly to His holy will and pleasure, and studying to serve Him in true holiness and righteousness all our days" (Exhortation at the time of Holy Communion).

It is because it is "our sacrifice of praise and thanksgiving" that the Liturgy or Service of the Lord's Supper is sometimes called the "Eucharist," or giving of thanks (1 Cor. xiv. 16).

3. **Charity.**—"And be in charity with all men." "Ye that are . . . in love and charity with your neighbours . . . draw

near" (Invitation to them that come to receive the Holy Communion). Charity, which means Christian love, is described in 1 Cor. xiii., and said to be the greatest of Christian graces. It is "the fulfilling of the law of duty towards our neighbour" (Rom. xiii. 8–11).

This qualification for worthy receiving brings before us another aspect of the Lord's Supper. It is "a sign of the love that Christians ought to have among themselves one to another" (Article XXVIII.). It is called in the Homily (second part, "Concerning the Sacrament"), "the mystery of peace," and "the Sacrament of Christian society, whereby we understand what sincere love ought to be betwixt the true communicants." It was immediately after its institution, and while still "at the table," our Lord gave to His disciples the "new commandment," "That ye love one another; as I have loved you, that ye also love one another. By this shall all men know that ye are my disciples, if ye have love one to another" (St. John xiii. 34, 35); thus associating love to one another with remembrance of Himself.

Unless, therefore, we possess this love, we cannot be true disciples of Christ or worthy partakers of His Supper (1 St. John iii. 23, iv. 20, 21).

The Lord's Supper is a *social* meal, as the title "Holy Communion" implies* a Communion or joint-partaking of the Body and Blood of Christ. "We," says St. Paul (1 Cor. x. 17), "being many, are one bread ('loaf,' R.V. margin), one body: for we are all partakers of the one bread (loaf)." †

"We shall know whether we be true members of Christ, and come rightly to the Lord's Supper, if, seeing in the Lord's Supper is contained

---

* Hence the importance of the requirement of our Church as to the number of Communicants in the Rubrics 2 and 3 at the end of "The Communion," and at the beginning of "The Communion of the Sick."

† "As this Sacrament seals up the communion of the members with the Head, so it seals up the communion of the members one with another. The Lord ordained these elements of such things, that being many in themselves, yet of many become one: bread is made of many grains of wheat, wine of many grapes, and yet the meal of those divers grains are moulded up into one loaf, and the wine of those several berries are pressed into one cup, to teach us that all the communicants at this Holy Table, how many soever there be, ought to agree together in one, like members of one body; as having one Father, one Faith, one Baptism, one inherit-

a token of friendship and love among men, we bear brotherly love to our neighbours, that is, to all men, without any evil will or hatred" (Nowell's Second Catechism).

Hence the importance of the directions in the Exhortation giving warning, "If ye shall perceive your offences to be such as are not only against God, but also against your neighbours; then ye shall reconcile yourselves unto them; being ready to make restitution and satisfaction according to the uttermost of your powers for all injuries and wrongs done by you to any other: and being likewise ready to forgive others that have offended you, as ye would (wish to) have forgiveness of your offences at God's hand;"* and also as to the duty of the Curate in the third Rubric before "The Communion."

In the Offertory, and Prayer for the Church Militant, we have illustrations of charity, and opportunities furnished for exercising, it in our prayers, and by our alms.

---

ance; as parts quickened by one and the same Spirit, brethren to be saved by one and the same Christ" (Bishop Nicholson's *Exposition of the Catechism*, Oxford, Parker, p. 195).

"As this broken bread was scattered upon the mountains, and was gathered together and became one, so may Thy Church be gathered together into Thy Kingdom from the ends of the earth" ("The Teaching of the Twelve Apostles," ix.).

* See St. Matt. v. 23, 24.

QUESTIONS.

1. Give a brief account of the history of the Church Catechism.
2. What is the Catechism intended to teach? How is it described in its alternative title, in the Baptismal Service, and in the Order of Confirmation?
3. Into how many parts may the Catechism be divided?
4. Why does it begin with "What is your name"? Show how the whole of the Catechism is connected with this question.
5. What is "a member"? Illustrate and explain from Scripture "a member of Christ," "the child of God," "an inheritor of the kingdom of heaven." Describe the privileges which belong to these, and show their relation to one another.
6. What three words describe the promises made in your name at your Baptism? How are these explained in the subsequent questions and answers?
7. What do you mean by "renounce"? How is this duty described in the Baptismal Service?
8. What sins are specially "the works of the devil"?
9. What do you mean by "this *wicked* world"; by "pomps and vanity"? How are these described in the Baptismal Service?
10. What is meant by "the Flesh"? What are its "sinful lusts"?
11. What is meant by "articles," "*the* Christian Faith"? Where are the "Articles of the Christian Faith" summed up?
12. What do you mean by "keep" God's holy will and commandments? "Walk in" ("the same"). What is "the same"?
13. Why do Christian privileges come before Christian duties? Give Scripture illustrations to show that this is the right order.
14. Why do you think that you are bound to believe and to do *as* your godfathers and godmothers promised for you? *When* are you bound thus to believe and to do? When do you publicly acknowledge this obligation?
15. What is the meaning of "this state of salvation into which you have been called"? What must you do in order to be saved? How can you do this?
16. What are the three great enemies of a Christian? Give an instance from the Bible in which each of these (1) overcame men, and (2) were overcome by men.
17. "Yes, verily, and by God's help so I will." What do you here declare your determination to do?

18. What do you mean by, "I believe in," "Maker of *heaven,*" "Jesus," "Christ," "His *only* Son"?

19. Explain from Gospel history the words, "Suffered under Pontius Pilate." Why is he named?

20. Explain and prove from Scripture, "He descended into Hell."

21. Explain the words "quick," "Catholic," "Communion," "Saints."

22. "The Holy Catholic Church." Explain these words fully, and illustrate your answer from Scripture. What is the connection of this clause with the article which precedes and those which follow it?

23. Show from Scripture that forgiveness of sins is promised through Christ, and that it is the office of the Christian Church and ministry to proclaim this offer; and upon what conditions it is promised.

24. "What dost thou chiefly learn in these Articles of thy Belief?" Write out the answer; and explain the words—"redeemed," "sanctifieth," (noting the change of tense), "all the world," "all mankind," "all the elect people of God." Give illustrations from Scripture.

25. In what respects do Redemption and Sanctification differ?

26. Prove from Scripture our worship of "One God in Trinity, and Trinity in Unity."

27. Give a proof from Scripture of each Article of the Creed.

28. "I am the Lord thy God which brought thee out of the land of Egypt," &c. What lessons does this Preface to the Commandments convey to Christians?

29. Write out "My duty towards God;" showing which part of it explains each of the first four Commandments.

30. In what short form of words, called the First and Great Commandment, are these Commandments summed up?

31. In which Commandments are we taught to "worship" God; to "honour His Holy Word;" to "serve" Him?

32. Explain the words "graven," "jealous," "visit," "thousands," "take in vain," "all that in them is," "hold guiltless."

33. How do the First and Second Commandments apply to us?

34. Why do Christians keep holy the first day of the week instead of the seventh?

35. How did our Lord explain "In it thou shalt do no manner of work"?

36. How did our Lord teach us that the Commandments are to be understood?

37. What sins are forbidden by the Third Commandment?

38. Point out the difference between the First and Second Commandments, and illustrate your answer from Scripture.

39. Write out "My duty towards my neighbour," showing which part of it explains each of the last six Commandments.

40. Who is my neighbour? How did our Lord teach this?

41. How should my love to God differ from my love to my neighbour? Whence does love to my neighbour proceed?

42. Explain the Fifth Commandment so as to show its general teaching, as given in "My duty towards my neighbour"?

43. What is the Fifth Commandment called in the New Testament? Who set an example of obedience to it?

44. What sins does the Sixth Commandment forbid?

45. What sins does the Seventh Commandment forbid?

46. How does the Tenth Commandment differ from the others? How does St. Paul speak of it?

47. Give in one word the principle laid down by each of the last six Commandments?

48. Which Commandments forbid (1) sins of the tongue, (2) sins of the hands, (3) sins of the heart?

49. Which Commandments forbid idleness, backbiting, gluttony, falsehood, quarrelling, cheating, murmuring, unbelief, superstition.

50. Which Commandments enjoin reverence, purity, contentment, diligence, kindness, truthfulness, loyalty?

51. Which Commandments contain (1) a threat; (2) a promise; (3) a reason?

52. Which Commandments warn us against (1) the lusts of the flesh; (2) the vain pomp and glory of the world; (3) the works of the devil?

53. What is the reason given in the Catechism for the insertion of the Lord's Prayer?

54. What are the uses of the Lord's Prayer? Show this by our Lord's words in giving it, according to the two Evangelists who record them.

55. Write out the question coming before the Lord's Prayer, and compare it with the answer to "Dost thou not think that thou art bound," &c. What important truths are taught in it?

56. Write down separately the clauses of the Lord's Prayer, placing under each the explanation given of it in "I desire."

57. By what petition of the Lord's Prayer are we taught the *measure* of the obedience we should strive after?

58. What is temptation? Why do we say, "defend us *in*," and not *from* all dangers?

59. Explain these words, "hallowed," "trespass," "special" grace, "diligent" prayer, "goodness," "ghostly."

60. What is prayer? Give a short account of (a) our Lord's practice; (b) His teaching as to prayer.

61. "Give us this day our daily bread." Give the explanation in the Catechism of this petition, and explain it fully.

62. Explain in the words of the Catechism the first three petitions of the Lord's Prayer. Which is a missionary prayer? What is the difference between "serve" and "obey"?

63. What does the name "Our Father" teach us? And what does "which art in heaven" teach us?

64. Against what "evils" should we always pray?

65. Explain the condition, "As we forgive them that trespass against us."
66. What is essential to the success of prayer?
67. What lessons are taught us by the petition, "Give us *this day* our *daily* bread"?
68. What may we learn from the order of the petitions in the Lord's Prayer?
69. "What meanest thou by this word Sacrament?" Write out the answer, and carefully paraphrase it.
70. What, then, are the necessary constituents of a Sacrament?
71. "Two only." Show from the definition of a Sacrament that those five commonly called Sacraments, mentioned in Article XXV., "are not to be counted for Sacraments of the Gospel."
72. Explain the words "generally necessary to salvation." Show from Holy Scripture that two Sacraments, and only two, are generally necessary to salvation.
73. Mention some instances in Holy Scripture in which the gifts of the Holy Spirit were given by means of an outward and visible sign.
74. What do you understand by the words "a sign," "a means," "a pledge"? Give illustrations of your answer from Holy Scripture.
75. When did our Lord ordain Baptism and the Lord's Supper, and in what words?
76. "In the name of the Father, and of the Son, and of the Holy Ghost." Explain the exact meaning of these words as used in the Catechism and in Holy Scripture.
77. What is required of persons to be baptized? Give the answer and prove it from Scripture.
78. Compare the answer "Repentance whereby," &c., with the account of the promises made in your name in answer to the question "What did your godfathers and godmothers then for you?"
79. What do you understand by "outward" and "inward"?
80. What does "repentance" mean? Give illustrations from Scripture of true and false repentance.
81. What are "the promises of God made in" the Sacrament of Baptism?
82. Quote from Scripture some of the promises made to repentance.
83. Illustrate from Scripture the following terms:—"A death unto sin," "a new birth," "children of wrath," "children of grace."
84. "Why then are infants baptized," &c.? Explain the answer to this question, substituting for the pronouns the nouns for which they stand.
85. By what name are sponsors called in the Catechism? What other names are applied to them? Why is their office retained in the Administration of Baptism, and what are their duties?
86. What arguments can be derived from Scripture in favour of Infant Baptism?

87. In what relation to the life of a Christian do Baptism and the Lord's Supper stand? Why is the latter repeated, but not the former?

88. "Why was the Sacrament of the Lord's Supper ordained?" Write out the answer, and explain the words "continual," "sacrifice," "thereby." What are the benefits we receive thereby?

89. What did the Lord command to be done with the bread and wine? Show this from Scripture.

90. What is the inward part or thing signified (in the Lord's Supper)? Explain the words "verily," "indeed," "faithful." In what manner are the Body and Blood of Christ given and received, and by what "mean"?

91. What is required in order to be a worthy partaker of the Lord's Supper?

92. What are the five subjects for self-examination suggested in the Catechism for those who wish to come to the Lord's Table?

93. Give quotations from the Catechism expressing the need for the life after Baptism being in accordance with the beginning made in Baptism.

94. Compare the two descriptions given in the Catechism of the blessings of Baptism.

95. How is it that Baptism is twice treated of in the Catechism? Explain separately, and show the substantial identity of the two statements, "Wherein I was made," &c., and "being by nature born in sin," &c.

96. What do you gather *from the* Catechism concerning the office and work of the Lord Jesus Christ?

97. How did God the Son redeem you and all mankind, and *from* what and *to* what did He redeem you?

98. What are the spiritual benefits of which the faithful are partakers in the Lord's Supper?

99. What is the inward and spiritual grace of the Sacrament of the Lord's Supper? Is this grace given unconditionally? Refer to Holy Scripture in support of your answers.

100. What does the Catechism say—(a) Was promised for you in your Baptism; (b) is required of persons to be baptized? Show that the two agree.

101. Name the Commandments which correspond to the first, fourth, and fifth petitions of the Lord's Prayer. Give the grounds of your answer.

SELECT LIST OF BOOKS
DEVOTIONAL AND PRACTICAL

PUBLISHED BY

JAMES NISBET & CO.

THE CHRISTIAN UNDER REVIEW.
A Series of Works on Practical Christian Life
Small crown 8vo.

THE CHRISTIAN'S INFLUENCE. By the Ven. WILLIAM MACDONALD SINCLAIR, D.D., Archdeacon of London. 2s.

THE CHRISTIAN'S START. By the Very Rev. the DEAN OF NORWICH. 1s.

THE MORAL CULTURE OF THE CHRISTIAN. By the Rev. JAMES MCCANN, D.D. 1s.

THE PATHWAY OF VICTORY. By the Rev. ROBERT B. GIRDLESTONE, M.A., Hon. Canon of Christ Church, and late Principal of Wycliffe Hall, Oxford. 1s.

THE CHRISTIAN'S RECREATIONS. By the Rev. HENRY SUTTON, M.A., Vicar of Holy Trinity, Bordesley. 1s.

THE CHRISTIAN'S PROGRESS. By the Ven. G. R. WYNNE, D.D., Archdeacon of Aghadoe. 1s.

THE CHRISTIAN'S DUTIES AND RESPONSIBILITIES. By the Very Rev. the DEAN OF NORWICH. 1s.

THE CHRISTIAN'S AIMS. By the Rev. ALFRED PEARSON, M.A., Incumbent of St. Margaret's Church, Brighton. 1s.

THE INTELLECTUAL CULTURE OF THE CHRISTIAN. By the Rev. JAMES MCCANN, D.D. 1s.

THE CHRISTIAN'S PRIVILEGES. By the Rev. W. J. DEANE, M.A. 1s.

THE CHRISTIAN'S INHERITANCE. By the Rev. C. A. GOODHART, M.A., Incumbent of St. Barnabas', Highfield, Sheffield. 1s.

"Simple and forcible as these books are in their teaching, and brief in extent, they deserve the attention of those who direct the religious teaching of the young."—*Scotsman.*

"We dipped into these pages alike with pleasure and profit. The writers, each on his own theme, seem steadfastly to keep in view scriptural teaching, sound doctrine, and the trials and temptations which beset the daily life and walk of the believer."—*Word and Work.*

"How completely they cover the field of Christian needs is sufficiently indicated by their titles. They are well fitted to stimulate the piety and clear the views of those holding the doctrines of the Church of England."—*Liverpool Mercury.*

By H. BONAR, D.D.

GOD'S WAY OF PEACE. A Book for the Anxious. 16mo, 1s. 6d. Cheap Edition, paper cover, 6d.; cloth, 9d. Large Type Edition, crown 8vo, 2s.

GOD'S WAY OF HOLINESS. 16mo, 1s. 6d. Cheap Edition, paper cover, 6d.; cloth, 9d. Large Type Edition, crown 8vo, 2s.

By MATTHEW HENRY.

EXPOSITION OF THE OLD AND NEW TESTAMENTS. With Practical Remarks and Observations—
In Nine Volumes. Imp. 8vo, £2, 2s. *Net.*
In Six Volumes. Medium 8vo, £1, 11s. 6d. *Net.*

By LADY CATHARINE LONG.

HEAVENLY THOUGHTS FOR MORNING AND EVENING HOURS. Selections in Prose and Verse, with Passages from Scripture. With a Short Introduction. 16mo. Cloth, 2s. 6d.; silk, 4s. 6d. each.

By HARRIET E. COLVILE.

THE WAY SHE TROD. A STUDY. Just Published. Small crown 8vo, 2s. 6d.

"'The Way She Trod' is a study of the development of religious sentiment and belief in a girl's character."—*Scotsman.*

FLOWER VOICES. With Illustrations. Demy 16mo, 1s.

WAFTED SEEDS. With Illustrations. Demy 16mo, 1s.

New Books by Dr. PARKER.

Crown 8vo, 5s.

WELL BEGUN. A Book for Young Men. By the Rev. JOSEPH PARKER, D.D., Author of "The People's Bible," &c.

NONE LIKE IT. A Plea for the Old Sword. By JOSEPH PARKER, D.D., Author of "Ecce Deus," and Minister of the City Temple, London. This book discusses the higher criticism from a preacher's standpoint, and gives reasons for accepting the Bible as the Word of God. The book welcomes the results of all capable and reverent scholarship, and endeavours to show that the orthodox view of the Bible, and the Evangelical conception of its doctrine, are beyond successful attack.

By Miss MARSH.

THE RIFT IN THE CLOUDS. Small crown 8vo, 1s.

CROSSING THE RIVER. Small crown 8vo, 1s.

SHINING LIGHT. Small crown 8vo, 1s.

WHAT MIGHT HAVE BEEN. A True Story. Crown 8vo, 1s.

By Rev. J. REID HOWATT.

THE CHILDREN'S PEW. Sermons to Children.

AFTER HOURS; or, The Religion of Our Leisure Time. With Appendix on How to Form a Library for Twenty Shillings. Small crown 8vo, 1s.

THE CHILDREN'S PULPIT. A Year's' Sermons and Parables for the Young. Second Edition. Extra crown 8vo, 6s.

THE CHILDREN'S ANGEL. Being a Volume of Sermons to Children. Crown 8vo, 2s. 6d.

By Miss NUGENT.

THE PRINCE IN THE MIDST. Jesus our Centre. 16mo, 1s.

By SAMUEL GILLESPIE PROUT.

NEVER SAY DIE: A Talk with Old Friends. 16mo. 9d.; paper cover, 6d.

By the Very Rev. W. LEFROY, D.D.,
DEAN OF NORWICH.

HOW DO I KNOW I AM A CHRISTIAN? Crown 8vo, 2s.

By Major SETON CHURCHILL.

BETTING AND GAMBLING. Small crown 8vo, cloth, 1s. 6d.

By the Rev. JAMES WELLS, M.A.

BIBLE OBJECT LESSONS. Addresses to Children. With Illustrations. Crown 8vo, 3s. 6d.

BIBLE ECHOES. Addresses to the Young. Small crown 8vo, 3s. 6d.

THE PARABLES OF JESUS. With Illustrations. Small crown 8vo, 5s.

BIBLE CHILDREN. Studies for the Young. With Illustrations. Small crown 8vo, 3s. 6d.

BIBLE IMAGES. With Illustrations. Crown 8vo, 3s. 6d.

By the Rev. J. H. WILSON, D.D.

THE KING'S MESSAGE. A Book for the Young. With Illustrations. Small crown 8vo, 3s. 6d.

THE GOSPEL AND ITS FRUITS. A Book for the Young. With Illustrations. Crown 8vo, 3s. 6d.

OUR FATHER IN HEAVEN: The Lord's Prayer Familiarly Explained and Illustrated for the Young. With Illustrations. Crown 8vo, 2s. 6d.

By EDITH RALPH.

STEP BY STEP THROUGH THE BIBLE. PART I. FROM THE CREATION TO THE DEATH OF JOSHUA. A Scripture History for Little Children. With a Preface by CUNNINGHAM GEIKIE, D.D., LL.D., and Twelve Illustrations. Crown 8vo, 2s. 6d.

FROM THE PREFACE.

"Miss Edith Ralph, in this little book, shows herself exceptionally skilful in her delicate task. . . . The tone and spirit of her pages seem to me admirably suited to her subject—simple, tender, gentle, wise, and full of sweet Christian love, they point the little ones invitingly to heaven, and lead the way. . . . Nor is the careful and well-informed intelligence wanting which is needed to make the first steps in Bible knowledge a preparation for safe and healthy progress in it hereafter."

Part II. FROM DEATH OF JOSHUA TO END OF THE OLD TESTAMENT. A Scripture History for Little Children. Revised and recommended by CUNNINGHAM GEIKIE, D.D., LL.D. Twelve Illustrations. Crown 8vo, 2s. 6d.

"No sweeter, wiser, or more Christian story of the Scriptures could be given to a little child or read to it."—*Christian Commonwealth.*
"Just the thing for Sunday afternoon."—*Word and Work.*

By FREDERICK A. ATKINS,

Editor of "The Young Man," and Hon. Sec. of the National Anti-Gambling League.

MORAL MUSCLE: AND HOW TO USE IT. A Brotherly Chat with Young Men. With an Introduction by Rev. THAIN DAVIDSON, D.D. Now ready. Small crown 8vo, 1s.

Dr. CLIFFORD writes:—"It is full of life, throbs with energy, is rich in stimulus, and bright with hope."

The Methodist Times says:—"An excellent book for young men—manly, honest, straightforward, and full of Christian earnestness."

FIRST BATTLES, AND HOW TO FIGHT THEM. Just Published. Small crown 8vo, 1s.

"An excellent book for young men. The addresses are vigorous and to the point. The work would certainly help to develop in a thoughtful reader truer manliness than generally prevails among our young men."—*Irish Ecclesiastical Gazette.*

"Another of Mr. Atkins' capital little books for young men."—*British Weekly.*

HOW TO STUDY THE BIBLE. By Dr. CLIFFORD, M.A.; Professor ELMSLIE, D.D.; R. F. HORTON, M.A.; Rev. F. B. MEYER, B.A.; Rev. C. H. WALLER, M.A.; Rev. H. C. G. MOULE, M.A.; Rev. C. A. BERRY; Rev. W. J. DAWSON. Third Edition. Small crown 8vo, 1s.

"In this little book we have the choicest counsels of men who are themselves successful students of the Word. We very earnestly commend this volume. All those who desire to know how to study the Scriptures with the utmost profit should secure it at once."—*Christian Advocate.*

"Young Bible students will find some very valuable hints in this little volume."—*Nonconformist.*

"The whole of these essays are well worthy of perusal, and are as instructive as they are interesting."—*Manchester Courier.*

"In this small book are comprised eight practical and, we may say, delightful essays from well-known divines and authors."—*Schoolmaster.*

THE QUESTION OF QUESTIONS: "WHAT THINK YE OF CHRIST?" By SAMUEL WAINWRIGHT, D.D., Incumbent of St. Stephen's, Clapham Park. Crown 8vo, cloth, 7s. 6d.

By Rev. THEODORE CUYLER, D.D.

STIRRING THE EAGLE'S NEST, AND OTHER PRACTICAL DISCOURSES. Just Published. Extra Crown 8vo, 6s.

"A volume of earnest and able sermons, full of life and vigour."—*Literary Churchman.*

HOW TO BE A PASTOR. Recently Published. Crown 8vo, 2s.

By the Rev. ALFRED PEARSON, M.A.,
INCUMBENT OF ST. MARGARET'S CHURCH, BRIGHTON.

CHRISTUS MAGISTER: SOME TEACHINGS FROM THE SERMON ON THE MOUNT. Just Published. Crown 8vo, 5s.

The Dean of Winchester says:—"A delightful volume: the chapter on 'Non-Resistance' pleases me especially."

THE CHRISTIAN'S AIMS. Small Crown 8vo, 1s.

By R. A. TORREY,
SUPERINTENDENT OF THE CHICAGO BIBLE INSTITUTE.

HOW TO BRING MEN TO CHRIST. Crown 8vo, 1s. 6d.

By FRANCES BEVAN,
AUTHOR OF "THREE FRIENDS OF GOD."

THE RIVER OF GOD. Crown 8vo, 3s. 6d.

BY THE
Venerable JOSHUA HUGHES-GAMES, D.C.L.,
ARCHDEACON OF MAN.

EVENING COMMUNION. Crown 8vo, 2s. 6d.

By the Rev. ANDREW MURRAY.

NEW BOOK.

BE PERFECT. A Message from the Father in Heaven to His Children on Earth. Meditation for One Month. Extra Pott 8vo, 1s.

Small crown 8vo, 2s. 6d. each.

THE NEW LIFE. Words of God for Disciples of Christ.

"This book stands out among many of its kind as distinguished by a new impulse and freshness of thought."—*Scotsman.*

ABIDE IN CHRIST. Thoughts on the Blessed Life of Fellowship with the Son of God. Sixty-third Thousand.

"The varied aspects of this practical truth are treated with much freshness, power, and unction. It cannot fail to stimulate, to cheer, and to qualify for higher service."—Mr. Spurgeon in *The Sword and Trowel.*

LIKE CHRIST. Thoughts on the Blessed Life of Conformity to the Son of God. A Sequel to "Abide in Christ." Twenty-eighth Thousand.

"The author has written with such loving unction and spiritual insight that his pages may be read with comfort and edification by all."—*Literary Churchman.*

WITH CHRIST IN THE SCHOOL OF PRAYER. Twenty-fifth Thousand.

"A volume of rare excellence, and one which is much needed."—*Christian News.*

HOLY IN CHRIST. Thoughts on the Calling of God's Children to be Holy as He is Holy. Tenth Thousand.

THE SPIRIT OF CHRIST. Thoughts on the Indwelling of the Holy Spirit in the Believer and the Church. Eighth Thousand.

Small Crown 8vo, 3s. 6d.

THE CHILDREN FOR CHRIST. Thoughts for Christian Parents on the Consecration of the Home Life. Tenth Thousand.

"There is a tone of fervour and devotion pervading the book that contrasts pleasantly with the trivially inane tone some writers think fit to adopt in writing for and about children. All Sunday-school teachers and parents would do well to lay its lessons to heart."—*Methodist Recorder.*

By the Rev. J. HAMILTON, D.D.

THE MOUNT OF OLIVES, and other Lectures on Prayer. 16mo, 1s.

A MORNING BESIDE THE LAKE OF GALILEE. 16mo, 1s.

THE PEARL OF PARABLES. Notes on the Parable of the Prodigal Son. 16mo, 1s.

THE LIGHT TO THE PATH; or, What the Bible has been to Others, and What it can do for Ourselves. 16mo, 1s.

EMBLEMS FROM EDEN. 16mo, 1s.

THE HAPPY HOME. 16mo. With Illustrations. 1s.

THE BLESSED LIFE: How to Find and Live It. By N. J. Hofmeyr, Senior Professor of the Theological College of the Dutch Reformed Church, Stellenbosch, Cape Colony. Small crown 8vo, 2s. 6d.

"The teaching is sound throughout, and expressed in vigorous language. —*Christian*.

"We have seldom read a book which gives such a grasp of Redemption in its purpose, as in its enjoyment by the individual, in so brief and compact a manner as the one before us. The treatment is suited only to an intelligent, if not educated, Christian. To such it is calculated to give an intellectual, as well as spiritual, perception of the things which accompany salvation."—*Rock*.

By the Rev. GEORGE MATHESON, D.D.

MOMENTS ON THE MOUNT. A Series of Devotional Meditations. Second Edition. Crown 8vo, 3s. 6d.

"This little volume is not one to be read through at a sitting, and then laid aside. Rather each meditation is to be pondered over, and enjoyed singly and separately, and to be dwelt upon until it becomes a permanent possession. Their suggestions can hardly fail to stimulate to Biblical and theological research."—*Scotsman*.

VOICES OF THE SPIRIT. Small crown 8vo, 3s. 6d.

"A choice little volume of devotional meditations. It is not only devout in spirit and tender in tone, but marked by freshness of thought, which volumes of this kind too often lack."—*Methodist Recorder*.

WISDOM'S HOUSE AND "HER SEVEN PILLARS. By Lady Beaujolois Dent. Small crown 8vo, 1s. 6d.

"An excellent little work, sound in doctrine, and thoroughly practical in its application to the reader's conscience."—*Record*.

LONDON: JAMES NISBET & CO., 21 BERNERS STREET, W.

www.ingramcontent.com/pod-product-compliance
Lightning Source LLC
Chambersburg PA
CBHW020146170426
43199CB00010B/904